The Patient Abuse and Neglect of Our Vulnerable Adults

The Patient Abuse and Neglect of Our Vulnerable Adults

✦

America's Shame

Joseph S. Bostwick
Former Special Agent, Office of the Inspector General, Washington, DC Government. Lead investigator Patient Abuse and Neglect Unit.

iUniverse, Inc.
New York Lincoln Shanghai

The Patient Abuse and Neglect of Our Vulnerable Adults
America's Shame

iUniverse books may be ordered through booksellers or by contacting:

iUniverse
2021 Pine Lake Road, Suite 100
Lincoln, NE 68512
www.iuniverse.com
1-800-Authors (1-800-288-4677)

Because of the dynamic nature of the Internet, any Web addresses or links contained in this book may have changed since publication and may no longer be valid.

ISBN: 978-0-595-47187-4 (pbk)
ISBN: 978-0-595-70946-5 (cloth)
ISBN: 978-0-595-91466-1 (ebk)

Printed in the United States of America

The depictions and opinions described in my book are presented in good faith and to the best of my memory and ability. They are based on my own long law enforcement career, training, experiences, notes, lessons, plans and, as stated, to the best of my memory. Although I proudly reference both the Maryland Office of the Attorney General and the Washington, DC Office of the Inspector General, in no way does this book represent any views or opinions of those respective government agencies.

To all the dedicated and talented prosecutors with whom I worked during this long journey. I thank you from my heart for your trust, support and guidance.

Contents

Foreword. xi

CHAPTER 1   Patient Abuse and Neglect: What Is It? 1

CHAPTER 2   How to Start up a Dedicated Unit or Patient
Abuse Coordinator (PAC). 18

CHAPTER 3   Suggested Checklist for the Investigation of Patient
Abuse and Neglect. 24

CHAPTER 4   Suggestions on What to Inform the Police. 31

CHAPTER 5   Key Facility Personnel and Records 36

CHAPTER 6   Pressure Ulcers/Decubitus Ulcers/Bedsores 46

CHAPTER 7   Suggested Methods of Interviewing Special
Witnesses and Elderly Victims. 53

CHAPTER 8   General Investigative Procedures for both Internal
and Criminal Investigations. 60

CHAPTER 9   Prevention. 96

CHAPTER 10   Things to Remember on the Road to Success 106

APPENDIX A 121

APPENDIX B 125

APPENDIX C 127

Acronyms 129

Glossary 131

Foreword

✦

The Patient Abuse and Neglect of Our Vulnerable Adults

In May of 1989, I was fortunate to be "in the right place and at the right time." I had recently retired from the Baltimore County Police Department, at the rank of Detective Sergeant, and was selected as a member of the Medicaid Fraud Control Unit (MFCU) in the Office of the Maryland Attorney General. The Maryland Legislature had just passed a revolutionary new criminal cite, The "Abuse or Neglect of Vulnerable Persons."[1] Visionaries such as Maryland's former Attorney General J. Joseph Curran, Jr. and others to include both governmental and private sector advocates realized the State of Maryland must and would start to address a growing problem, the criminal abuse and neglect of vulnerable adults. In the early 1980s, the State of Maryland took similar steps to pass legislation to address the criminal neglect and abuse of children. At that time I was also in the right place and at the right time. At that time I was supervising three units one of which was the Child Abuse Unit. It was an exciting time to be involved in the efforts to protect our victimized children. In the spring of 1989, shortly after joining the Medicaid Fraud Control Unit (MFCU), I was presented with another opportunity to protect the vulnerable. Attorney General J. Joseph Curran, Jr. issued an internal communication to all staff of the Medicaid Fraud Control Unit, which had authority to investigate and prosecute Medicaid Fraud occurring in facilities receiving Medicaid funding, would now take on the investigation and, when appropriate, criminal prosecution of allegations of patient abuse or neglect of our vulnerable adults. A "vulnerable adult" under Maryland law means "an adult who lacks the physical or mental capacity to provide for the adult's

---

1. Original Criminal citation: Art. 27, 35B and amended 35D. Present cite is Annotated Code of Maryland, "Abuse or neglect of a vulnerable adult," First and Second Degree, and Abuse or neglect of a vulnerable adult-Investigation, sections 3-604, 3-605 and 3-606.

daily needs." These citizens often need assistance with all their activities of daily living (ADL), that you and I take for granted, such as eating, walking, toileting, and dressing, etc. These vulnerable citizens also need our protection from those caregivers who subject them to the various forms of abuse.

After the announcement by Attorney General J. Joseph Curran, Jr., it was clear that the Medicaid Fraud Control Unit must embark on a journey into uncharted waters. The law was brand new and we had received the mandate to investigate, and when appropriate prosecute allegations of patient abuse or neglect, occurring within Medicaid-funded facilities, however, with no additional prosecutors or criminal investigators. The teams within the MFCU, which consisted of a prosecutor, an auditor and an investigator, were already burdened with heavy case loads. In addition, while we all knew we would be taking on these new cases, no staff had come forward to "take the banner" and move forward, except one new guy to the office. The new guy, a retired detective sergeant, had taken on several fraud cases and thanks to the assistance of others in the unit, specifically, Peggy Gayhardt and Terry Collins, managed to investigate and assist the legal staff in the successful prosecution or adjudication of several criminal Medicaid Fraud cases. However, the new guy had many years of criminal investigation experience, some of which was assisting in the protection of other vulnerable persons. After obtaining permission from his supervising Assistant Attorney General the new guy, your writer, submitted a written plan proposing that the MFCU devote one full-time investigator to be assigned all patient abuse and neglect cases. This would be a major undertaking since we had no real models or action plans to follow. We had no data base, no investigative policies and procedures. We had no contacts with others in the investigative "loop" such as the Department on Aging (both State and local Ombudsman), State Department of Health, law enforcement agencies, and long term care providers. To add to the challenge, the Medicaid Fraud Control Unit was not even included in the "loop" of mandated notification should allegations of patient abuse or neglect occur. We would have to set up a dedicated unit within the MFCU since it was my opinion, and still is, that patient abuse and neglect cases don't mix well with criminal fraud cases. They are like water and oil. Fraud cases take many months and require extensive review of the financial records, etc. The patient abuse world would be fast and, at times, furious.

My report to our legal staff recommended that the Patient Abuse Investigator be a full-time position and that the person assigned must want to work these cases and not merely be assigned at random. The investigator would need to travel state-wide when deemed necessary. The office would, in time, and after conferring with the local prosecutors, take on cases wherever the investigative roads would lead. In short, the investigator, later titled Patient Abuse Coordinator, would be on the road a great deal of the time and be able to make investigative decisions at times without close supervision by his assigned Assistant Attorney General. The investigator would have to reach out to those already in the reporting loop, the State Department of Health, the Long Term Care Ombudsman, and law enforcement agencies across the state. Law enforcement officers are critical to any criminal case, since they are often the "first responders." Their initial report can often make or break a later more in-depth criminal investigation.

The police, respectfully, were the least equipped to actually "investigate" patient abuse or neglect cases. They were and still are uncomfortable within the confines of the "nursing home world." They were previously trained simply to file a basic report and "get back on the road" to take more calls. Sadly, and police will tell you, they feel more like professional "report takers" than criminal investigators. I say this with all respect, and please recall your writer retired from one of the largest agencies in the country. The others in the mandated reporting loop, the State Health Department and Long Term Care Ombudsman, had decades of experience at their level investigating regulatory cases of abuse or neglect of vulnerable adults. This was not lost on the Office of the Attorney General. In fact, the first two "outreach" calls I made were to them. In short, we had to start from the "bottom up." We had to successfully perform various "start-up" activities and request that reports be sent to the Patient Abuse Coordinator—Office of Attorney General. We had to be trained and offer training to others in the loop. In short, the challenge was not only to "sell our product," but also to back it up with successful investigations and victories in court. We had to accomplish all this and again, with no additional personnel. Over the years and after very hard work our office would be the leading prosecutorial agency. In fact, the Office of the Attorney General would take the "banner" and still holds it high today.

The Patient Abuse Coordinator assisted our legal staff in providing information and training to other prosecutors around the state, since local Offices of the State's Attorney also have jurisdiction to prosecute patient abuse and neglect cases, and at times they will proceed, for which they must be commended. They often did not, and often still don't, have a dedicated investigative unit assigned to handle these cases within their respective jurisdictions. One example is a case in the mid-1990s which had been reported as occurring in Baltimore County. This is one of the largest populated regions in the State of Maryland. (Please note we will not use the actual names of victims, locations of the alleged incidents or the identities of the suspects and/or defendants.) The case involved a very elderly and mentally impaired female resident of a respected Long Term Care Facility (LTCF). Due to both mental and physical infirmities the reported victim, who had sustained visible injury, could not provide information to the police or others in the investigative loop.

The case reached District Court Level (Maryland's lower court), after the loving daughters of the victim gathered information on their own and applied for a "Statement of Charges" (Charging Document) through a District Court Commissioner. In short, the local prosecutor had no case. The patient did sustain visible injury, but with no witnesses this could be explained away by alleging another patient inflicted it. The defendant was a Licensed Practical Nurse (LPN) employed by an agency. I often refer to agency staff as "phantom care givers", since they come and go from facility to facility making no bond with other staff or patients under their care. The defendant denied the allegations and was prepared to proceed. However, as we have discussed, the local prosecutor could not proceed with a criminal case. He was about to request that the judge "Nol Pros" the case (i.e., drop the charges) for its clear legal flaws. A Long Term Care Ombudsman politely gave the prosecutor my business card, while suggesting he refer the case to the Office of the Attorney General. The prosecutor did. We opened our own case, conducted our own in-depth investigation, and gathered necessary medical and personnel records. We then applied for a Statement of Charges backed up with our findings and evidence, took the case to trial and our legal staff prevailed. This is an example of how reaching out and establishing professional rapport with other agencies can pay off and pay off big.

When I reference certain actions or results of investigations and trials I do so to the best of my memory and through the personal notes and papers, which I have kept over these many years in the various units I have served. Specifically, the supervisory and management position of Detective Sergeant in the Baltimore County Police Department, the Maryland Office of the Attorney General, as the "first" Patient Abuse Coordinator, and the Office of the Inspector General for Washington DC, as a Special Agent and the first Lead Investigator of their newly formed Patient Abuse and Neglect Unit.

As I have often said, our legal staff took on cases others would not. They did the right thing in seeking justice. Although I would travel down the long and dusty road or, in some cases, the jungle to gather evidence for the legal staff, they won the cases. I just carried the evidence into the courtroom. Respectfully, the legal staff I was honored to work for and with are Maryland's former Attorney General J. Joseph Curran, Jr., who first committed the Medicaid Fraud Control

Unit to the investigation and, when appropriate, prosecution of allegations of patient abuse and neglect state-wide. In addition to all his other duties and responsibilities, Attorney General J. Joseph Curran, Jr. kept a very keen interest in the protection of our vulnerable adults. The former Director of the Medicaid Fraud Control Unit, Gale E. Rasin, presently a Circuit Court Judge, accepted my written and rather bold proposal to commit one full-time criminal investigator to pursue allegations wherever the road may have lead. In short, a revolutionary full-time commitment. This was in 1989, when we first created, designed, and later carried into the affray, the "banner" we will address in this book. Her former Assistant Director, Daniel Anderson. In the "early days" Dan was my biggest advocate. He also had my name placed into a nomination pool of other national candidates for consideration to attend the "Certified Instructor's Course," conducted at the Federal Law Enforcement Training Center (FLETC), Glynco, GA. This later provided me and other successful graduates the opportunity of presenting training nationwide on the investigation of allegations of patient abuse and neglect. Dan also lead the unit and later continued his career in federal service. Carolyn J. McElroy, as the Director of the Unit, "continued the march" of the commitment by, among other things, designating the lead investigator position as the Patient Abuse Coordinator or PAC. Now enter the patient abuse and neglect prosecutors, the ones who stood and delivered in open court. Assistant Attorney General (AAG) Timothy X. Sokas was the very first MFCU prosecutor assigned patient abuse and neglect cases along with his extensive docket of fraud cases. This was a critical time for our efforts since we were the "new kids on the prosecutorial block." Once we got out there, worked some cases, and took a few to court, the investigative and prosecutorial "wheel" started in motion and continues to this day. AAG Timothy U. Sharpe was the first AAG to actually get out there in the field with me occasionally when appropriate. Under his guidance we kept extending the investigative and prosecutorial net wider and wider across Maryland. (I wish we had "frequent driver miles," but it was great and rewarding!) We entered courtrooms that had never seen AAGs in action! Tim Sharpe went on to a corporate position with a national company. He and his wife Lori still keep in touch. Tim and the next AAG on our list, Catherine Schuster Pascale, accounted for the largest number of successful prosecutions. AAG Catherine Schuster Pascale picked up the ball from Tim Sharpe and we didn't miss a beat. The "net" grew still larger and larger and so did the number of successful prosecutions, and they were statewide. AAG Catherine Schuster Pascale is still out there holding the "banner" high as I write this book. There is no finer prosecutor of these cases out there, period. Cathy and her husband Kevin also still keep in touch. In fact, I have consulted Cathy during the writing of this book. Last, but of course by no means least, is Office of the Inspector General for Washington, DC, Attorney Alexis Taylor. What can I say about Alexis Taylor? In just one year we set up a Patient Abuse Unit for the OIG of Washington, DC. Alexis and I had to duplicate everything I and Maryland's legal staff had accomplished. We had a brand new law, although we were "in the reporting loop" by law, we were still breaking new ground with all the other agencies in DC. In just 12 months we established a professional rapport with all those in the loop, started working and winning cases, and in the end we had done it! We had ourselves an up-and-running Patient Abuse Unit with hundreds of referrals, numerous open cases and five successful prosecutions. One extensive investigation and successful prosecution (Involuntary Manslaughter) involved the tragic death of a long term care vulnerable adult. Alexis is one of the finest persons I have ever known. She still devotes her services to the people, but in another government office. Although not "legal staff," I must give honorable mention to two persons who were also instrumental in the overall success of our efforts for the DC Office of the Inspector General. They are Investigator Elizabeth Collette, who was a key member of our "little unit" and Mr. Gerald Kasunic. Jerry is a nationally known Long Term Care Ombudsman assigned to protect and serve as an advocate for the vulnerable adults of the District of Columbia. In Maryland? Where to start and where to end? I wish I had more space to name them all, but you know who you are and I thank you from the bottom of my heart for your assistance. However, I must mention Maryland's legendary State Long Term Care Ombudsman, Ms. Patricia Bayliss, who is still out there as we speak, and the former head of the Nursing Home Unit within Maryland's Department of Health and Mental Hygiene, Mr. James Ralls. James now holds a key position within the Centers for Medicare and Medicaid Services (CMS). Lastly, I must give credit to my friend and mentor David Carman, Chief Investigator (ret.), Delaware Medicaid Fraud Control Unit. Dave and I worked for many years providing nationwide training to members of other State Medicaid Fraud Control Units (SMFCUs). He is a true gentleman and a friend to this day. Dave will be mentioned in the "Sources," since, at times, we produced lesson plans together.

In the courtroom, the investigator's role is that of another "witness." During my over 11-year tenure as Maryland's first Patient Abuse Coordinator and one year tour of duty as a Special Agent—Lead Investigator within the Office of Inspector General—Medicaid Fraud Control Unit, Washington, DC, I reviewed over 3,000 referrals, conducted over 300 open investigations, testified in court, testified before the Grand Jury, testified before state law makers regarding legislation, and assisted our legal staff to proceed in 88 criminal trials and/or other successful adjudications, with a total of only 3 defeats. I was honored to be the recipient of numerous awards and citations from both the government and private sector, to include, upon retirement from Maryland State Service, "The Governor's Citation." I was also very pleased to have been commended by the citizens I served by receiving over 50 complimentary letters. However, it is the legal staff that stands up and delivers in the courtroom. My role especially in the beginning, was to cut a path through the jungle of cases, recommend we proceed or not proceed, establish and maintain a data base, travel the entire State of Maryland working cases, testify in court, train others in the system and keep the lines of communication open. A well-established Patient Abuse Unit should transcend personnel changes. While I was honored to be named by Attorney General J. Joseph Curran, Jr., via a performance award, as "The Founder of the Patient Abuse Unit," the unit lives on as it should. I was honored to walk into any court with any of our prosecutors knowing we did the "right thing" protecting our vulnerable citizens. You see, after all, those medically or mentally infirmed are still our "citizens." They were once working moms during World War II. They were doctors, nurses, attorneys, clerks, clergy, brick layers, physical therapists, various craftsman, United States Marines and other warriors and heroes, professors of great and noble disciplines, and yes, criminal investigators and retired detective sergeants. Simply, they were once what we are today.

At the same time we were networking, we had to begin responding to the complaints and when appropriate, go throughout the State wherever the road may lead and take one and win it. The more we reached out the more complaints or referrals we received and the more cases we selected for criminal investigation. You see, we could not just "talk" about patient abuse and neglect; we had to back our "words" with "actions," such as successful criminal prosecutions and/or other forms of adjudication. In my initial report to the Director of the Medicaid Fraud Control Unit (MFCU), I suggested we first reach out to one of the largest counties in Maryland, Baltimore County, which at the time had over 50 nursing homes. This did not count retirement homes or providers for the developmentally disabled adults or DDA providers. Maryland's criminal cite protects not just our vulnerable residents of "nursing homes," but also what I would later call, "the hidden iceberg" of allegations of abuse or neglect occurring in group homes and centers for mentally disabled adults. At times, our open cases in group homes actually out numbered active cases in nursing homes or long term care facilities (LTCF).

In 1989, we reached out to the Baltimore County Police Department, Central Records, and requested that the department start to copy the Office of the Attorney General—Patient Abuse Coordinator on all allegations of abuse and neglect occurring in county facilities. In addition, we requested copies of all such reports filed for the previous year (Statute of limitations was 1 year.). Thankfully, the police department complied with our request. As a result, our office received 48 police reports. One, and only one, fit the profile for appropriate action by our prosecutors.

However, it was nearly one year old and the "clock was ticking." Allegations had been made that a male caregiver sexually abused several male clients. However, as the Patient Abuse Coordinator, I would say and still do say in training sessions conducted nationally, "Patient abuse and neglect can happen in any facility and at any time." Our legal staff authorized the investigation, because it was the "right thing to do." To say it was not a strong case is an understatement. We knew going in that the case had many flaws such as the alleged victims could not testify and we had no actual "eye witnesses" to a specific criminal act. However, we had no "fatal flaws," such as the violation of the suspects Constitutional rights. At most, we had a "circumstantial" evidence case in the form of other caregivers who had come forward stating that they had found the suspect caregiver in the rooms of male "clients" (patients) under very suspicious circumstances. This suspect had been seen repeatedly by numerous staff caregivers in the private rooms of mentally disabled "clients" very late at night sitting on their beds. This was also behind closed doors. The suspect was not conducting any form of standard care and, of course, his care did not necessitate that he sit in bed with a "client," especially behind closed doors and at night. Our office felt the victims deserved some type of appropriate response.

Keep in mind, especially you attorneys and law enforcement officers out there, with all the flaws we still chose to proceed. After numerous interviews of staff, the gathering of medical records, etc., we found the suspect caregiver working in a State of Maryland facility for developmentally disabled clients. He had been terminated from the other private facility. In the "early days" of these cases, termination of employment was often the means by which facilities dealt with accused employees, but follow-up by prosecuting authorities was not common. Some suspect caregivers applied for positions at other facilities and were hired "on the spot." Why? Human Resource units often did not conduct proper verifications or reference checks on applications. Also, at the time, the State of Maryland did not have a law requiring that criminal history checks be conducted on caregivers and other specified employees. Thanks to Attorney General J. Joseph Curran, Jr., and others this would change.

However, I digress, and this is another chapter in the long and winding road of these cases. After three "non-custodial interviews" the suspect caregiver admitted to the sexual abuse of one patient. The final interview was conducted by this writer and the legendary fellow investigator, Jerry Landsman. I need not describe the specific acts other than to say that they did not result in any evidence of physical injuries. And all physical evidence, such as sheets and blankets, etc., had long been sanitized by the facility laundry. The case was the very first successful prosecution of a patient and neglect related case in the State of Maryland. It was proper that it was prosecuted by our office. The rest, as they say, "is history." Receipt of reports and referrals took off like rockets and the big wheel started turning and has never stopped. Eventually, as Patient Abuse Coordinator, I had ongoing cases in all parts of the State of Maryland, and the unit still does today.

The purpose of my book is to provide information to law enforcement officers, investigators, legal staff, government regulatory agencies and the providers of care, on proven and tested methods on how to conduct criminal and administrative investigations into allegations of the patient abuse and neglect of our vulnerable adults. My book is also beneficial to various medical professionals, such as doctors and nurses, especially in the geriatric specialties since they must learn to recognize and prevent incidents of patient abuse and neglect of vulnerable adults under their care and supervision. Administrators and medical professionals working in the arena of providing care to our mentally disabled vulnerable adults will also benefit from the information in my book. Other caregivers included in this category of "need to know" are home health care workers of all the medical disciplines. Remember, the patient abuse and neglect of our vulnerable adults also occurs in private homes. As the reader travels from chapter to chapter in this book he/she will find examples of what I refer to as "real cases and real faces" from my many years in this field. My book also provides valuable information to the families and responsible parties of their vulnerable loved ones in facilities across our country. The issue of the patient abuse and neglect of our vulnerable adults will only become more prominent in the decades to come. Why? "Baby Boomers" will flood the health care and long term care facilities (LTCFs), and Skilled Nursing Facilities (SNFs), and other care settings across America within the next 15-20 years. My book is also the memoir of the long and dusty roads I traveled during my 35 year law enforcement career.

Joseph S. Bostwick—Summer 2007 Baltimore County, Maryland

Retired Detective Sergeant Baltimore County Police Department
Former Special Agent, Washington, DC Office of the Inspector General
Retired State of Maryland Employee: Office of the Attorney General—"Founder of the Patient Abuse Unit" (via an award from Attorney General J. Joseph Curran, Jr.)

1

Patient Abuse and Neglect: What Is It?

As I have often stated during training presentations, patient abuse and neglect are many things to many people, but always the same to the victim. What I mean by this is that they have different "meanings," different "responses" and different "responsibilities" for different people, such as the State Health Department, the Long Term Care Ombudsman, the Providers (nursing homes and other types of facilities), and Law Enforcement, also to include the respective State Medicaid Fraud Control Unit—Patient Abuse Unit. However, to the victim the crimes of abuse and neglect are always the same. The victims don't care about different "definitions" and different "responses," etc. They just know that they have been victimized, and mostly likely will be victimized again. They need help and need it sooner not later. National statistics over the years kept by the Long Term Care Ombudsman (LTCO) have also revealed a significant number of alleged incidents of abuse or neglect goes unreported by the victims and by staff. We also must mention the mentally incoherent victims, to whom I refer as the "permanently silent victims." These patients can't come forward to articulate their accusations. Finally, as in Maryland, a lot of States also have specific criminal cites for patient abuse and neglect. In Maryland, the criminal cites for patient abuse and neglect are in the same law book as murder, arson, and rape, etc. These are criminal acts and will be prosecuted as such. Caregiver staff and other employees must know this.

One key here is for providers to report allegations of abuse and neglect in a timely manner, not just because there might be some State law or regulation, but because it is the right thing to do. Other keys to success are that those government agencies charged with the response and investigation of these allegations do so rapidly and also keep each other informed of findings in an accurate and timely manner. For example, I always looked upon the Long Term Care

Ombudsman, who as you may know are most often citizen volunteers, as my "eyes and ears" within the facility. There were never "too many" calls from the Long Term Care Ombudsman's Office as far as I was concerned.

There are often time limits to "report" allegations of abuse and neglect, but 24 to 48 hours to report, for example, can be a lifetime to the alleged victims. These victims are often physically and mentally impaired. Witnesses can fail to come forward and injuries can start the healing process. Of course, this can lead to repeated abuse and neglect even before a required reporting requirement is met by the facility. There are also reporting requirements among government agencies in the reporting "loop" (State Health Department, Long Term Care Ombudsman, Providers and Law Enforcement).

Patient abuse can come in the forms of "abuse" or a "battery." It can come in the form of "neglect" or in the intentional failure to provide for the patient's basic needs, such as food, water, hygiene, etc. Criminal Neglect can result in such insidious conditions as pressure sores (AKA Decubitus Ulcers or bedsores)[1], which come in four stages, which can and do lead to serious and long-lasting medical conditions and also death. We will address this matter in more detail later in this book. Patient abuse can also come in the form of "Emotional Abuse." In some States, emotional abuse (screaming and yelling at patients, name calling and ridicule, etc.) are "criminal acts." Regardless, this type of patient abuse is aggressively investigated and pursued by regulatory agencies such as the State Health Department and Long Term Care Ombudsman, as well as the care providers themselves.

Patient abuse can also come in the form of "financial abuse" or simply put the misappropriation or theft of monies belonging to vulnerable adults. Some cases would include the theft of Social Security or other social program benefits. One case we had occurred in a group home for mentally impaired vulnerable adults. The primary investigator in our Unit assigned to this case was one of our Medicaid Fraud Investigators, who was also a paralegal, determined that large amounts of money allocated for the "residents" of the group home was actually being diverted for the personal use of caregiver staff. Mentally disabled vulnerable adults were "on the books" as being provided personal computers and very expensive brand name sporting goods. All of which could not be used by the developmentally disabled patients. Auditors must be vigilant in the tracking and verification of purchases to eliminate such cases of financial abuse.

---

1.   For purposes of convenience, I shall refer to these simply as Pressure Sores.

One of the most insidious forms of patient abuse is when it occurs in the form of Sexual Assault or Rape. Yes, sexual predators also roam the halls of nursing homes and other locations caring for our vulnerable adults. States have their own respective definitions and elements for the crimes of Sexual Assault, Sex Crimes and Rapes, but I think we all know what they mean not only to us but to the vulnerable adult victims. You may recall early on in this book that I thought that as a retired detective sergeant in one of Maryland's largest law enforcement agencies, that I had seen it all. You may also recall I stated that I was wrong. Not only did this revelation occur while working my patient abuse cases of assault and neglect etc., but it really hit home when our Sexual Abuse cases started coming in. In fact, you may recall earlier I reported that the very first case ever prosecuted in Maryland related to our patient abuse and neglect laws was the sexual assault committed by a male caregiver on a developmentally disabled male adult. I would later have other cases.

I will report on a case here that is yet another example that "Patient abuse and neglect can happen in any facility and at any time." This incident occurred in a respected "chain" nursing home located in NW Baltimore County, Maryland. It was not late at night or on a holiday weekend, etc. This incident occurred in broad daylight, on a weekday and within fifteen feet of the rest of the world. Two Nursing Assistants were at a work station which happened to be directly across from a room in which two female patients resided. The female patients had been diagnosed with Alzheimer's disease, and were nonverbal. It was during AM care and the facility hallways were busy with both patient and caregiver traffic. One of the patients in the room had a visitor, her brother. The two Nursing Assistants took note that while the door to the room was opened the "privacy curtain" was closed around the geri-chair of one of the patients. Geri-Chairs are recliners on wheels serving multiple purposes in a Long Term Care Facility. (LTCF). The privacy curtain was not around the patient who had a visitor, it was around her roommate. In fact, the legs of the male visitor could be seen standing near the head level of the other patient. The two Nursing Assistants thought that the visitor was attempting to provide some type of assistance to his sister's roommate. Since this was their job, they entered the room unannounced. When they pulled the privacy curtain aside they were shocked to find the male visitor having the demented female patient performing a sex act on him. Not only was the suspect a "visitor," he was 84 years old! However, once we established that he was mentally and physically competent to stand trial, his case was presented to the Grand Jury and he was indicted. Successful prosecution by our legal staff followed. Sadly, there were other cases. What is most important in these types of cases is that the patient be treated and protected as a victim of a crime and that the location of the alleged sexual assault be treated like the "crime scene" it is. This takes extensive training of the medical staff and administrative staff of the locations of the offense but also the police. Often, police seem to leave most of their law enforcement skills at the front door of the nursing home. While things have improved over the years, some police officers just don't feel comfortable investigating allegations of patient abuse and neglect. We will discuss this issue later. I'm certain our law enforcement officers out there will benefit and in fact feel more confident and comfortable investigating the growing criminal acts of patient abuse and neglect after reading this book.

Finally, those responsible for the investigation of these allegations, be they regulatory or criminal investigatory agencies, must never forget that no matter their individual responsibilities, they must be clear and united in the fact that the protection of alleged victims is paramount. The victims don't care about different regulations and laws, jurisdictions and such; they just want and deserve our protection.

Please note, of course, each State has their respective Laws and Regulations pertaining to the allegations of patient abuse and neglect. We will address this matter in a generic but informative manner. It should also be noted that I will lace this book with cases I have worked over these many years to illustrate the elements and types of abuse and neglect. This book is not about statistics and graphs. It provides insight into the "Patient Abuse World," as I refer to it. Before we proceed I must also mention here that most nursing homes and other facilities caring for our vulnerable adults are good and pleasant places to care for our vulnerable adults. It must also be noted that being a caregiver is a difficult and challenging job, but it does not justify abusing patients. However, most caregivers do a fine job under challenging conditions and without just compensation. Again, this does not justify crossing the line from having "a bad day" to being a "criminal."

Patient Abuse

Patient abuse comes in many forms and many degrees but most often comes in the form of a physical attack or "battery." (Some examples are slapping, punching, kicking and the pulling of the ears and hair, etc.) In short, a physical attack upon a vulnerable adult under the care of an assigned caregiver. Note: In some rare cases, we even encountered suspects who were not caregivers, but "visitors" and even "volunteers."

An example of one of our "real cases and real faces" was the early criminal investigation and prosecution of a local metropolitan fire department Emergency Medical Technician (EMT). This is also an example our legal staff not being afraid to take on the tough cases. The patient, whom I will never forget, was 101 years of age and demented. However, up to the date of the alleged incident she was still ambulatory. I will explain. The victim had sustained a fall inside her own room and it was clear to medical staff present, including the DN and other registered nurses, that the victim had sustained a hip fracture. The facility called "911" and an ambulance arrived with two male EMT personnel. The alleged patient abuse, (Assault & Battery), occurred as the two aforementioned male EMTs were in the victim's room. The victim had not been moved pending their arrival. Keep in mind before we go on that at the time of this alleged incident the following facility staff were witnesses: the DN, several other RNs and CNA staff. We had numerous professional level eye witnesses. Well, it came to pass when one of the male fire department EMTs knelt down beside the thrashing and clearly in pain 101-year old victim. As one of the male EMT staff was conducting the assessment, the arm of the demented victim came up accidentally knocking off his hat. What was the response of this trained medical professional EMT in question? Why, it was to immediately grab the victim by her throat with both his hands, while saying words to the effect "Don't ever do that again!" All the witnesses screamed and were mortified. The suspect EMT's own male partner had to intervene on behalf of the victim.

Our office was notified in a timely manner by the DN, with whom we had already established a professional relationship. It was also clear that while the fire department was conducting an internal investigation, the local prosecutor's office was not going to place criminal charges. Why? Who knows? Some thoughts come to mind such as the fire department would most likely take disciplinary action and plus the cold hard fact that even with the alleged act, the age of the demented victim, and the numerous professional eye witnesses to include the suspect's own partner, the prosecution of fire fighters, as well as police officers, can be tough cases at trial.

After some discussions, our office decided to take on the case because, although risky, it was the righteous thing to do for the helpless victim. We took the case to the Grand Jury and in rapid time they returned multiple count Indictments against the suspect fire fighter EMT.

At trial, we presented everything possible for victory. We had medical records establishing that the victim was a "vulnerable adult," the written statements of the numerous eyewitnesses, and all our follow-up investigative findings and evidence. We had a case! Later in this book you will read how I rarely provided the suspect notice I was coming to conduct his/her interview and just as rarely provided them their Miranda Warnings. However, if I was informed they had an attorney, there was no interview. Although extremely rare, this is what occurred in this case. The suspect informed me he had an attorney who had advised him not to talk with me. Thus, I had no chance at him. No matter, we had a ton of evidence, right? The jury was out on the case less than 45 minutes before returning an acquittal on all accounts! Why? We did manage to poll a few who advised very clearly that we had indeed presented a very strong case against the defendant. However, in the end, they just could not bring themselves to convict a fire fighter. Please, being in government service 35 years and also a citizen, I have the deepest respect for police officers and fire fighters, but not as far as this particular jury took it. Bottom line, the case was one of only three cases our office lost in the over 11 years I was the Patient Abuse Coordinator. We will address the others as the book continues. This case is an example of many things but most of all an example that juries do what juries do. It is our system of justice.

It is key to the investigation of these types of cases to take photographs of the injuries alleged to have been sustained as a direct result of the abuse. At times the facility does not take photographs but documents the injuries in Progress Notes. This is fine, but when you stand before a jury with Progress Notes they lack the impact of color photographs. Often the victims can't or won't come forward because of fear of retaliation by the caregivers. Also, fellow caregivers have a documented history of not coming forward "proactively" to report such attacks and also are reluctant witnesses when testifying before the Grand Jury and in Court. In my experience photographs can at times be paramount in winning criminal cases due to the powerful effect photographs taken contemporaneously to the alleged incident have on the jury.

Be alert for patient abuse being hidden under the veil of injuries of unknown origin. I am very aware that injuries of unknown origin can and will occur in nursing homes and other facilities providing care to vulnerable adults. However, having extensive experience via thousands of reports of abuse or neglect, I can firmly tell you that acts of intentional abuse have and will continue to be hidden under the veil of injuries of unknown origin. This occurs most often when the abuse or physical attack happens without reliable witnesses. One example is for some unjustified reason such as being spat on or slapped by the vulnerable adult patient the caregiver responds with a slap or punch, etc. In any other environment this would be an Assault & Battery, but in the patient abuse world what we are addressing here is a classic criminal response by the caregiver—suspect. If a visible injury results and is surely going to be found by another caregiver on the shift it occurs or the next shift, then the caregiver files a false report in order to "veil" the criminal act the caregiver has intentionally committed. Often used examples are that the suspect "found" the injury and/or it must have been done by another staff or even another patient. There can be "patient to patient" incidents of battery and such, but if they are both demented, and most are, the matter is not for the police or prosecutor but for the facility and/or regulatory agencies to address. However, in some cases, it can also merit a criminal investigation because of the possibility of "Criminal Neglect" by staff for failing to provide proper supervision of their patients.

Another form of patient abuse being hidden under a "veil" is patients sustaining injuries as a result of an accident. The origin is truly an "accidental" injury sustained to the patient-victim by the caregiver-suspect. An example: A caregiver transfers a patient from geri-chair to bed. The caregiver knows that the Care Plan, which he/she has signed off on, requires that the patient have two caregivers conduct the transfer. However, as usual, the caregiver is short on time and long on patients and performs the transfer alone. However, without malice or intent, the caregiver drops the patient and the patient sustains a visible injury. Perhaps the patient does not sustain a "visible" injury. Of course, the profile of the patients-victims in these cases indicates that they are unable to speak for themselves due to physical or mental infirmities. What I have repeatedly advised caregivers, during training or interrogations over the years is don't commit a criminal act and indeed become a "criminal" just because you made a mistake and dropped the patient by accident, causing, injuries or not. It is far better to report the incident and be disciplined administratively rather than have a "mug shot" added to your lifetime of photographs.

Visible injuries sustained as a result of such acts are bad enough; it is the unreported incidents that don't display visible injuries that pose even greater danger to the patient. Why? Example: The caregiver assigned to the next shift following an unreported accidental injury caused by a prior caregiver, responds to the patient's room to conduct normal care and "finds" that the victim has a very swollen leg or arm. The limbs may even appear to be fractured. As any doctor or nurse will tell you, there are no such things as "just fractures" when they are sustained to elderly vulnerable adults as they can lead to very serious conditions and even be the cause of death. Any caregiver who has an accident with their patient, causing visible injuries or not, must report the incident in a timely manner. **Period.** In Maryland, this type of patient abuse and neglect would fall under the definition of Criminal Neglect, since the caregiver failed to provide for the medical care and treatment of a patient under his/her care.

Another form of patient abuse and neglect is the Sexual Abuse or Assault of a vulnerable adult by a caregiver. Yes, as we addressed earlier in this book, even in nursing homes and group homes for the developmentally disabled, sexual predators can roam. Sexual Abuse will be addressed in more detail.

PHYSICAL AND CHEMICAL RESTRAINTS

Patient abuse can also come in the form of improper and unauthorized implementation of physical and chemical restraints. Patients have the right to be free from unauthorized physical and chemical restraints. In the past, it was all too common to observe physical and chemical restraints implemented not because of any documented medical need, but rather for the convenience of caregivers as a form of supervision and control. Nursing homes or other care settings must ensure that the right to be free of the unauthorized implementation of physical or chemical restraints is not violated. Government surveyors, as well as Long Term Care Ombudsman, also look for such violations during the inspection of the facility.

Physical Restraints

A physical restraint is anything that is attached to or placed next to the patient's body that limits his/her movement or access to his/her body. Physical restraints include leg or arm restraints, hand mitts, vests, cloth ties (bed sheets ties), wheelchair safety bars, or anything else that prevents patients from moving around. Other ways to restrain are moving the patient's wheelchair against a wall so that it cannot move, using a bedrail, or tucking in the bed sheet so tightly that the patient cannot move. Trays locked in place across patients' in "geri-chairs" can also act as a form of physical restraint. Nursing homes are prohibited from restraining patients or from doing anything that limits the patient's movement unless the patient, or the patient's responsible party, gives them permission.

A restraint may only be used to treat a patient's medical symptoms and only if the restraint will assist the patient in reaching his/her highest possible functioning. Before a facility can implement the use of physical restraints the facility must attempt other methods of treatment that exclude restraints. One example would be to provide the patient with therapy to improve his/her ability to stand and/or walk. Staff may attempt lowering the bed to the floor, thus, limiting the chance of falls and the serious injuries that may result. I have seen an extra mattress placed next to the bed to act as a preventative measure from falls. I have also seen double or single mattresses placed directly on the floor. Thus, if the patient accidentally rolls out of bed he/she simply rolls onto the floor or better another mattress. The facility may also use innovative methods of the placement of pillows and pads on or around the patient's body to assist in the prevention of accidental injuries.

If the various proper methods implemented have failed, it is time for the intervention of a doctor. Some of the steps the doctor may take before his/her medical interventions are to review the patient's chart and to meet with nurse management. If medically necessary, the doctor will write an order for the appropriate restraint.

Chemical Restraints

Chemical restraints are any drugs, not required or authorized, that are used for convenience and, sadly at times in the past, discipline. These types of violations of patient's rights are utilized not for any proper medical need or symptoms. I am sure there are those out there with experience in this field, who recall the over-medication of patients as a form of control, supervision and mere convenience.

The nursing staff can't administer a drug to the patient or implement a physical restraint unless the patient or his/her representative grants permission. The nursing staff can't administer a chemical restraint or implement a physical restraint except for limited periods of time in cases of some type of emergency, where the patient could be in danger of harming his/herself or others.

A doctor must write an order and make official entries into the patient's chart providing instructions for nursing staff to follow in the administering of medications which act as forms of chemical restraints. The medical chart must clearly indicate the proper dosage and duration of the "chemical restraint."

Patient Neglect

Patient neglect is much more complicated than the more common forms of patient abuse such as the hitting or slapping of a patient. Patient neglect can be a single act of neglect by a single caregiver or it can be a systemic problem throughout the facility. Neglect, as we stated, can be "hidden" and thus very insidious. Please keep in mind individual States may or may not have its specific definitions of "Patient Neglect." Thus, we will address it in a generic manner or basic forms. What I can tell you is that "Neglect" cases require much more time to investigate compared to a simple "assault" on a patient. I do not mean to slight the standard patient abuse or Assault & Battery, but neglect cases often require the gathering of extensive medical records, multiple interviews of management and of medical staff in the forms of doctors, various experts and nursing staff. Criminal Neglect is intentional and systemic. It can occur over a period of weeks, months or sadly years.

One of the early and paramount criminal cases our office, Medicaid Fraud Control Unit of the Maryland's Office of the Attorney General, headed then by Attorney J. Joseph Curran, Jr., made involved a physician—owner of a deplorable long term care nursing home in Baltimore City, Maryland. Over an extended period of time management intentionally neglected patients by cutting back on nursing staff, Director of Nursing (DN), turnover was high as well was other nursing staff, and the basic frontline caregivers, Nursing Assistants. Cleaning materials were also slashed. Food stuffs were slashed. It even reached the point where towels and wash clothes were slashed. Caregivers were washing patients with white socks. It was our sincere hope that at least the white socks were clean. Everything cut back lead to the tragedy one would expect. Patients lost extensive amounts of weight; patients suffered skin breakdown and pressure sores resulted; injuries to patients occurred and often went unreported to senior medical staff. It was the classic "end result." Our office successfully prosecuted this case and the doctor in question was imprisoned.

Patient Neglect means the "intentional" failure to provide for the basic assistance for the physical needs of a vulnerable adult. Some examples are:

1. Food

2. Clothing

3. Toileting

4. Essential medical treatment

5. Shelter

6. Supervision

To provide additional insight here I will provide some true case examples.

Food: Each patient has a daily requirement of nutrition as determined by his/her Care Plan. Younger and healthier adults can skip a meal now and then, and/or go without proper nutrition without causing the long range and dangerous consequences sustained by vulnerable adults. If food is intentionally withheld or if the patient is improperly fed by a caregiver the negative consequences can be very serious and in some cases fatal. We had a case where, again a caregiver had too many patients and not enough time to provide the proper feeding of a patient under her care. The suspect caregiver's answer was to, in short, "force feed" the patient by literally jamming the food down the patient's throat. This could have resulted in the choking or even death of the patient but fortunately did not. However, the patient did sustain lacerations to her mouth and throat. Again, the caregiver knew the incoherent patient's Care Plan. This criminal case was both a form of "abuse" (Assault & Battery) and a form of "neglect" since the victim did not have the opportunity to ingest the proper amount of nourishment.

The criminal case against this suspect caregiver was successfully prosecuted by our legal staff, the Assistant Attorney Generals assigned to the Medicaid Fraud Control Unit. I can not give these prosecutors enough credit. We often took on criminal cases other jurisdictions chose not to move on. Our criminal cases were not handed to us on "silver platters." Nor did we just take on the so called "slam dunks." **(There are no such things as criminal case "slam dunks.")**

Clothing: A true case example of this type of neglect occurred when an incident was reported wherein the caregiver, as a means of discipline, took a wheelchair-bound and incoherent patient, and placed the patient outside the facility without proper clothing, and supervision, not to mention the uncalled for "discipline" issue, occurred in the winter.

Toileting: Some examples of this type of "neglect" are when a patient repeatedly uses the call light requesting assistance in getting to the bathroom. After repeated calls and failed responses by the caregiver or other staff nature takes over and the patient has an "accident." This can lead not only to additional neglect, since at times the caregiver, as punishment will not provide assistance to the patient in cleaning up the "accident" simply because the patient had the accident! This is serious enough, but what this can lead to can be devastating to the self esteem of the patient and to the breakdown of skin integrity, thus, causing or contributing to pressure sores. Pressure sores (bedsores), are not only often avoidable but can be life threatening in the more serious stages. We will address pressure sores in more detail later in this book.

Essential Medical Treatment: Examples of this type of "neglect" border on some of the above cited examples. (The doctor who cut back on almost all the essential medical equipment and staff as previously cited.) However, specifically some examples here are when the caregiver intentionally fails to provide medications to the patient. In some cases this can take on the form of the caregiver's diversion of the patient's medication for his/her own use, such as in narcotic based drugs, etc., thus leaving the patient in increased and avoidable pain. This form of patient abuse and neglect can also occur when medical staff fail to provide the patients the proper necessary medications in order to save operating costs.

Shelter: In short, what the word states is "shelter." To intentionally place a vulnerable in the outdoors for no legitimate purposes, thus exposing the vulnerable adult to the dangers such exposure presents. True case example: Our office took on a case which had reportedly occurred in a Long Term Care Nursing Home located in a Washington, DC suburb. The allegations involved the improper discharge of a medically and mentally infirmed, wheelchair-bound patient, who was also subjected to lack of proper shelter and supervision. The case displayed several classic criminal neglect elements of crime all in one case.

The facility had a change in management. New management had reviewed the records of an elderly, medically and mentally infirmed patient who was pending Medicaid status. The victim's attorney, who resided in Washington, DC, was attempting to liquidate the patient's assets and clear her for Medicaid eligibility. The patient owed the facility over $52,000. The new management informed the DN (Director of Nursing) that the patient would be discharged immediately. When the DN attempted to explain that this would not be possible and in violation Maryland and Federal regulations, she was again advised to carry out the orders. But where would the patient be taken? After the improper discharge, which occurred in the winter month of December, the patient was improperly transported in the personal van of the DN, which was not equipped to safely transport a wheelchair-bound patient. And where did they take the disoriented patient? Why, where else, to the front porch of her attorney! The attorney in question, who had no clue that his client was coming his way, lived in Washington, DC, some 45 minutes from the nursing home.

When the "caregivers" arrived at the attorney's home they left the patient on the front porch. She was in her wheelchair, wearing light clothing. Her personal property was stored in trash bags and strewn around her wheelchair. The caregivers then simply drove away leaving the previously described helpless patient. Of course, the attorney called 911 and the patient was transported to a DC hospital. Our office was notified the next morning. This writer and a seasoned State Health Department Nurse—Surveyor responded to both the hospital and the nursing home.

Of course, we already knew we had a serious regulatory case on our hands since this was clearly a tragic case of "Patient Dumping," but that was a matter for the State Health Department and not the Office of the Attorney General. Although the case seemed to "scream" for criminal prosecution, we had legal flaws that were indeed "fatal" for a criminal prosecution. At the time, Maryland's criminal cite for the "Neglect" portion of our patient and neglect law required "malicious intent." It also required "serious physical injury" be sustained to the victim. Fortunately, for our victim she did not sustain serious physical injury nor did she sustain any injury. We held discussions with our legal staff to determine whether or not to file charges of "Reckless Endangerment." In the end, however, we opted to file a very detailed investigation with the State Health Department which resulted in multiple administrative actions.

This case was a landmark one for our Patient Abuse Coordinator because it would lead to our testimony before the Maryland Legislature and our patient abuse and neglect law was amended. J. Joseph Curran, Jr. our long time Attorney General, with me gratefully by his side, testified before Maryland's General Assembly petitioning that the "Neglect" section of our law be amended as a direct result of this "landmark" case. Maryland's criminal cite was later successfully amended. It was an example of how, at times, lack of criminal prosecution can still result in the "right thing."

Supervision: This is one of the more common forms of "neglect" and also one of the more dangerous. Simply put, this act occurs when vulnerable adults are left alone without proper supervision. For instance, some developmentally disabled vulnerable adults must have 24-hour, "one-on-one supervision." Although over the years we had numerous such cases, several true case examples are paramount . In one case the assigned caregiver to three mentally disabled vulnerable adults removed them from the group home in which they lived and took them to her private apartment. The caregiver had no caregiving reason to take the victims to her apartment. It was strictly for her personal convenience. She had personal business to take care of and the victims had to be left alone for some time. Her answer was to take them to her apartment. (The caregiver risked detection leaving the victims alone in the group home.) It should also be noted that these particular victims were blind and deaf, nearly completely helpless souls. The caregiver placed a large bowl of food on the floor and gave each victim a spoon. She then left them completely alone. This was violation enough, but even worse, the apartment caught fire while the caregiver was gone! Fortunately, although shaken and having sustained some smoke inhalation the victims survived. Needless to say our office investigated and prosecuted this case.

I will provide a second example because of the old phrase about "lightening never striking twice in the same place." Our office had yet another case very similar to the above-mentioned one. It was a Friday morning and our office permitted casual dress on Fridays, caseload permitting, I was getting dressed and watching the early morning news coverage regarding a fire that had occurred over-night. The location was described by the newscaster as a "nursing home." The reporter explained how five mentally disabled patients had been left alone by their caregiver. While the caregiver was gone, the nursing home caught fire. The victims were saved due to a sprinkler system and timely arrival by the local fire department. The lone caregiver to the five victims was not on the premises of the "nursing home" upon arrival of authorities. Of course, what the story was covering was a "group home" for the developmentally disabled and not a "nursing home." Regardless, it was an allegation of criminal neglect at the very least. I called the office leaving a voice mail advising that I was responding to the case. Off went the casual and on went the suit. Our investigation revealed that the assigned lone caregiver received a call from her boyfriend who needed a ride from a mall which was about 40 minutes away, one way. Again, the answer to the problem of being in two places at once was for the caregiver to leave her patients alone, while she went to the assistance of her boyfriend. No problem, right? Before she left her assigned patients alone and without supervision, the caregiver thought it would be a good thing to light a few scented candles since the group home had a strong odor of urine. (She could have solved this problem without candles by taking out the trash!) The candles were placed too close to some curtains which caught fire. The caregiver left in such a rush that one of the five patients who needed assistance with most of her activities of daily living (ADL), was left on a commode. The victim was still sitting on the commode when rescued by the fire department! Again, sprinkler systems saved the day. As stated, upon the arrival of the fire department the caregiver was nowhere to be found. Our investigation later revealed that when the caregiver returned back to the group home and saw all the fire department response, she simply fled. Needless to say, our office aggressively investigated this case and it was successfully prosecuted by our Assistant Attorney General, (Multiple count criminal case of Criminal Neglect and Reckless Endangerment).

Before we move on I feel compelled to provide one more case example of criminal neglect, "real cases and real faces" in the form of supervision. A nursing assistant in a Long Term Care Nursing Home was providing personal care to her patient in the form of bathing. It must be noted that this caregiver had been assigned to this patient for two years and signed off numerous times on the patient's Care Plan, the plan of care as determined by medical staff. The victim was very elderly, blind, deaf, under 90 lbs. and lacked any mobility. When I testified before the Grand Jury I described the victim as "infant-like." The caregiver was employing the use of a special tub which along with hygiene provided the patient with water therapy. The patient was placed in the tub by the caregiver and soap was added to the rising water therapy. The caregiver had to return some personal phone calls. Again the caregiver's answer for being in two places at the same time was to do the following. The caregiver pulled the privacy curtain shut and also closed the tub room door, which was directly off a hallway. Although there were other tubs in the room only one was in use. Thus, leaving the infant-like and helpless patient unsupervised in the rising water of the tub. Some time later another employee assigned to House Keeping noticed water seeping from the tub room into the hallway. When the house keeper entered the tub area and pulled the curtain aside she was horrified to find the patient below water. Within moments, trained medical staff responded but all efforts to revive the patient met with negative results. Later the cause of death was determined to be drowning. I mentioned that the suspect caregiver had signed off on the patient's Care Plan for a reason. The Care Plan clearly documented that under no condition was the patient ever to be left unsupervised during such care that in the end resulted in her death. Again, our case was presented before the Grand Jury and along with patient abuse and neglect, a Manslaughter indictment was retuned.

To add to this tragedy, the defendant in the aforementioned Involuntary Manslaughter Case was also charged by our office for the Assault & Battery of a vulnerable adult female in another nursing home! Please recall this example when, later in this book, we address the systemic failure of some Human Resources personnel to fully and accurately investigate and verify Applications of Employment and Resumes.

Please note, we will again discuss the various forms of "patient abuse and neglect" when we reach Chapter Eight of this book. The discussions will be covered during our addressing of Criminal Investigations and Internal Investigations. As throughout this book our discussions will, when appropriate, be laced with "real cases and real faces."

Some Contemporary Reports of Interest

If one may think that "patient abuse and neglect" issues are not "contemporary," or even in our "future," I respectfully refer the reader to the CONSUMER REPORTS article entitled "Nursing Homes BUSINESS AS USUAL." Briefly, the story covers the fact that "two decades after the passage of a federal law to clean up the nation's nursing homes, bad care persists and good homes are still hard to find."

"Our investigation found that the state agencies responsible for overseeing nursing home care have often failed to correct problems. But consumers can increase their odds of choosing a good nursing home if they narrow their search to certain types. Our findings: Not for profit homes are more likely to provide good care than for-profits, based on our analysis of inspection surveys, staffing and quality indicators. The same analysis shows that independently run homes are more likely to provide good care than chains. Through its influence in politics the industry has whittled down the protection of the 1987 federal law."[2]

GAO REPORT DATED MARCH 2007

Throughout my career and in this book I have repeatedly addressed the cold hard fact that the issues of patient abuse and neglect of our vulnerable adults will not just "go away" and that we, meaning all the various government agencies and citizens must be ever diligent in our efforts to protect our vulnerable.

Now comes the United States Government Accountability Office report to the ranking member of the Committee on Finance, The Honorable Charles E. Grassley, of the U.S. Senate.

We have all heard the phrase, "A picture can be worth a thousand words." Well, in the case of the very title of the aforementioned GAO Report, one can clearly state that the "title" is worth a thousand words! Under the general heading of Nursing Homes follows, "Efforts to Strengthen Federal Enforcement Have Not Deterred Some Homes from repeatedly harming residents." While the very title and report that follows are disturbing enough I find the words "Repeatedly Harming Residents", especially offensive. The GAO report is 100 pages long and very detailed, but I will provide some highlights for the reader. [3]

"Why GAO Did This Study"

"In 1998 and 1999, GAO reports concluded that enforcement actions, known as sanctions, were ineffective in encouraging nursing homes to maintain compliance with federal quality requirements: sanctions were often rescinded before being implemented because homes had a grace period to correct deficiencies. In response, the Centers for Medicare & Medicaid (CMS) began requiring immediate sanctions for homes that repeatedly harmed residents. Using CMS enforcement and deficiencies data, GAO (1) analyzed federal sanctions from fiscal years 2000 through 2005 against 63 homes previously reviewed and (2) assessed CMS's overall management of enforcement. The 63 homes had a history of harming residents and were located in 4 states that account for about 22 percent of homes nationwide."

---

2.   "Nursing Homes: Business as Usual." Consumer Reports. Summer 2006, p. 38.

3.   GAO Report # GAO-07-241, March 2007.

"What GAO Recommends"

"GAO recommends that the CMS Administrator (1) develop an administrative process for collecting civil money penalties more expeditiously and seek legislation to implement this process effectively, as appropriate; (2) strengthen CMSs immediate sanctions policy: expand its oversight of homes with a history of harming residents; and (4) improve the effectiveness of its enforcement data systems. CMS generally concurred with GAO's recommendations." Please see the entire GAO Report # 07-241 for complete details. ("Provider" publication—American Health Care Association dated May 2007)

Now we do have yet another report this time by the above cited informative "Provider" monthly publication of May 2007. In this very detailed report "Provider" advises that "Customer Satisfaction Scores Improve." (National Survey Marks Gains in Quality of life.") The report measures such things as, Quality of life, Quality of Care and Quality of Service. In part, the report reads, "More than 75 percent of nursing facility customers are satisfied with the quality of life care, and service at their facility—with scores for quality of life topping 80 percent-according to a nationwide customer satisfaction survey of more than 92,000 patients and family members representing nearly 3,000 nursing facilities in the 50 states and the District of Columbia." The report is very detailed complete with graphs and charts. Please see "Provider" issue of May 2007. (**It must be noted here that I make reference to the above-mentioned articles as "think documents" only, and in no way do I personally endorse any or all of the articles findings.**)

2

How to Start up a Dedicated Unit or Patient Abuse Coordinator (PAC)

The investigative body, be it criminal, regulatory or even provider level, must address the issues of allegations of patient abuse and neglect on a full-time basis. In most cases, in the regulatory or provider worlds, they already have professionals assigned to this effort. Of course, this is often not their only responsibility, since most of these professionals are nurses (Directors of Nursing). Suffice to say, they possess a high degree of intelligence and "willingness" to properly pursue, investigate, and forward, good basic and sound investigations or "Incident Reports" to those in the loop such as regulatory agencies and law enforcement, to include the Medicaid Fraud Control Units. Regulatory personnel from units such as the Health Department have dedicated professional staff, who are often also nurses, who investigate abuse and neglect allegations along with their duties as nursing home surveyors. Regardless, the problem should be addressed on a "daily" basis, and not just when a complaint is filed. The PAC must be "proactive." If the case is of a criminal investigative level the investigator should not be merely "assigned" cases at random, but be a full-time commitment on the part of management. Ideally, the assigned investigator should "want" the full-time assignment as this will be a positive effect on in the total commitment by management.

It is also a positive element if the investigator or PAC has extensive experience in law enforcement. Some say this need not be "etched in stone," but extensive experience in the investigation of criminal activities is, in my opinion, a must. It not only has a positive effect in the outreach efforts with law enforcement and others, but provides the legal staff with the benefit of the criminal investigators experience. Many law enforcement staff can offer previous supervisory and management experience in law enforcement. Prior law enforcement staff are also used

18

to being "on the road" and with, at times, little supervision in making investigative decisions.

The assigned prosecutor should also "want" to be assigned these cases since without dedicated legal staff the PAC and/or other criminal investigators are "toothless tigers." In my case, this positive effect started at the very top of the Office of the Attorney General for Maryland, Attorney General J. Joseph Curran, Jr. I was very fortunate to have been assigned prosecutors who were very dedicated and supportive of our efforts. We had a well coordinated effort from the very first and it continues all these years later. The PAC needs to be out there in the field at all times of the day or night and throughout the State. The PAC must be available by pager and cell phone on a 24 hour basis. Please recall, once again that the crimes of patient abuse and neglect happen in facilities at any time, and they don't occur just on the "day shift." Thus, at times the investigators will have to travel long distances and work outside the "9 to 5" work day. This would especially apply to caregiver staff such as nursing assistants who can be difficult to locate for interview once out of the facility. Responding in a timely manner, and while the nursing staff are still in the facility, will save time and also provide time sensitive clarity. Of course, this does not imply that the patient abuse investigator acts on his/her own or is a "lose cannon," but an investigative asset that does not require close or "hands on" supervision at every part of the investigation by his/her supervising prosecutor. Finally, as in any investigator/prosecutor relationship, "trust" must be earned and then maintained.

In the case of regulatory investigative units, such as the State Local Health Department and Long Term Care Ombudsman, they often have professional staff such as nurses who know their way around the nursing home and can be a significant benefit to a criminal investigator. In most cases the personnel assigned to investigate "in house" or file "Incident Reports" are nurses along with senior staff of the facility such as the Administrator. At times, the criminal investigator will be fortunate by having the opportunity to work with an administrator who is also a nurse. I was fortunate to have this occur several times over the years. Finally, a full-time investigator, especially previously in the law enforcement arena, will be in a better position to reach out to and establish professional rapport with not only those in the law enforcement community but other government regulatory agencies. There must be in force a standard method of receiving referrals and complaints. Each incoming complaint or referral must be assigned a permanent tracking number in a data base maintained by assigned computer staff. The PAC should be willing and capable of providing cross-training to others in the "loop" such as law enforcement, Health Departments, Long Term Care

Ombudsman and even providers. Training facility providers can have a very positive effect on the efforts to give them the tools to properly document allegations of patient abuse and neglect. Through training and interaction, the PAC can give providers the solid "building blocks" for the foundation of a case. Other agencies providing additional building blocks are law enforcement, Health Department and Long Term Care Ombudsman. The PAC should have at least one personal direct link with others in the loop. This need not be in person but by any and all other forms such as email, cell phone, facsimile or other electronic means. The full-time Patient Abuse Coordinator must be "connected." These links and professional rapport are part of a never-ending cycle since personnel come and go and also the laws and regulations are subject to amendments.

The PAC, or Patient Abuse Unit ideally should have assigned to it or at least have access to, a registered nurse. Some Medicaid Fraud Control Units have been successful in this effort. The PAC must be able to navigate in the stormy waters of the long term care and developmentally disabled facility worlds. He/she must be familiar with the various facility records necessary for these cases and also with Patient Charts, etc., but he/she will also need the expert review of complicated medical records and assessments located in the various files that a registered nurse can provide. Over the years we also developed professional rapport with specialists such as Wound Care Specialists. These nurses must undergo extensive specialized training and pass very difficult written and practical tests. Pressure sores will be addressed later in this book.

In summary, the "start-up" needs a dedicated effort from the very top down, and must be maintained in order to carry "the investigative and prosecutorial banner." In the case of the Attorney General's Office of Maryland this continues as it did from the very beginning in the spring of 1989.

As stated, in 1989, I thought I had seen everything and "done" everything after my retirement as a detective sergeant. However, the patient abuse world was not only new to me it was relatively new to other agencies. The other agencies in "the loop" did, however, have some experience and noted accomplishments in their respective fields. One of the first things I had to accomplish was to reach out and establish professional rapport with other government agencies and also private sector agencies to include nursing homes, and other forms of caregivers. While the Maryland Office of the Attorney General under the leadership of then Attorney General J. Joseph Curran, Jr. and his legal staff had established an excellent reputation in such arenas as the prosecution of Medicaid Fraud cases, and Consumer Protection, etc., in 1989 patient abuse and neglect was just out of the gate and ripe for someone to take the challenge and move on these very time sensitive investigations. The very first thing I did after being given the responsibility of heading the investigative phase of the prosecution of patient abuse and neglect of vulnerable adults, was to reach out to others in "the loop" to inform them of our entry into the effort and request their assistance. It must be stressed that one of the first hurdles we had to clear was the fact that "by law" the Office of the Attorney General was not in the Maryland regulatory statute "requiring" that it be notified of a suspected patient abuse or neglect accusations. Others in the "loop" such as the Long Term Care Ombudsman, the State Department of Health, and the police were. We had to step up and inform them respectfully that although not in the mandatory reporting "loop" we wanted to be via professional rapport. This was no easy obstacle since nobody needs another government agency to notify or just "more red tape." Along with not being in the mandatory reporting regulations, the Office of the Attorney General also had to respect that local prosecutors also had the legal right to investigate and prosecute allegations of patient abuse and neglect, occurring in their respective jurisdictions. Due to some diplomacy and the fact that the local offices of the State's Attorney had and still do have huge court dockets, our assistance was more than welcomed.

We had to be proactive, as in the "early days," no one was going to come to us with anything. We were the new kid on the block. We had to do more than "talk" in time we were expected to "produce" results and numerous results at that. After calling the Long Term Care Ombudsman and State Health Department we set up regular meetings to bring our office up to date on the problem state-wide. We were trained and also provided training. While we never actually reached the level of "joint investigatory teams" we did at times work cases together to a certain point and then broke away to address our respective missions. The key to the success of any Patient Abuse Unit, along with a dedicated Patient Abuse Coordinator and the supervision of his/her legal staff, is the establishment of permanent professional relationships with others "in the loop." Without establishing and then permanently maintaining professional rapport with the other government agencies and even the providers, the Patient Abuse and Neglect Unit or PAC will fail.

The last mandatory reporting agency in Maryland is the law enforcement. Again, our Office was not in the reporting loop. It was absolutely paramount that our office reach out to law enforcement agencies through out the State of Maryland, as it will be to your agency should you establish a Patient Abuse Coordinator or Unit. You may recall in my "Foreword" that the very first case ever prosecuted in Maryland related to patient abuse or neglect occurred in Baltimore County Maryland. Thanks to the positive response of the Baltimore County

Police to our "verbal" request for copies of all patient abuse and neglect cases reported as occurring during the past calendar year. In that mass of reports was one and only one worth investigative follow-up. It was the "diamond in the rough" sort to speak that launched the patient abuse and neglect efforts of our office. So, in the very beginning we reaped the benefits of establishing a positive rapport with law enforcement. Of course, being a State agency, we could not stop with just one jurisdiction. So we marched on and on carrying the "banner" to every corner of the State of Maryland. We are not "Texas" to say the very least, but this was still no easy task. However, during the months and years to follow we met the challenge.

Why is law enforcement so important? Police are the very "first" criminal investigatory responders. State Health Department and Long Term Care Ombudsman Office personnel, while having expertise in various regulatory and nursing standards, are not police officers. They can not determine probable cause to believe a crime has been committed and make arrests as appropriate. Police can collect and preserve physical evidence, such as taking photographs. Law enforcement written reports, if done thoroughly, can be the strong building blocks for a criminal case to follow.

If however, the police report lacks the necessary information for follow up, they can be a hindrance rather than an asset. An example of "hindrance" is a case reported as occurring in one of Maryland's largest jurisdictions and thus largest police agencies. The entire report in question was one page and in fact was less than one paragraph total. The alleged incident occurred in a Long Term Care Facility (LTCF) nursing home. It was alleged that the mentally and physically infirmed patient had been slapped several times about the face. The original police officer filing the report advised that he responded to the location and spoke with RN "Smith."RN "Smith" advised that no injuries were sustained to the victim. The police officer then wrote in his report that he had spoken with RN "Smith" and that since the RN had advised no injuries were sustained to the victim that his report would be marked as "Unfounded." To the point, my above-mentioned summary is longer than the original police report. First of all, Maryland's criminal cite for patient abuse and neglect did not require that "physical injury" be sustained to the victim. Secondly, what about good old Assault & Battery? Keep in mind, nowhere in the report was it written that Assault and Battery or Patient Abuse did not happen, just that there were no injuries sustained.

In addition, the police officer based his entire report on his interview of RN "Smith." The police never interviewed staff or made contact with the victim. In short, this specific report is an example of everything a police report should not be. A word here about the victims seems in order. Unless I was advised by a doctor not to make contact with victim, and I was never told not to, I always attempted some type of contact with the victim, no matter what his or her medical chart indicated. First of all I wanted to see any physical injuries with my own eyes. I also wanted to take photographs, and lastly it was a way for me to give the victim the courtesy. Remember, these victims were once everything we are today and, in many cases such as mine, more. If the victim was indeed incoherent as described in his or her Medical Chart, I simply made an entry along the lines of, "Today, I attempted to speak with the victim. However, due to medical and mental infirmities, as documented in his/her Medical Chart, I could not communicate with the victim."

Of course, if physical injuries were alleged to have occurred to the victim as a direct result of the alleged patient abuse and neglect, I took my own set of photographs and placed them into our Evidence System. You might have noticed that we have not discussed an "Evidence System" in this book, nor will we. I could write a book just on evidence procedures alone. Suffice to say, any criminal investigatory agency, to include the Medicaid Fraud Control Units, must and do have a formal evidence system, which must document the arrival of evidence, in whatever form, into the custody of the Evidence Control Unit. The system must also document such paramount facts as the "Chain of Custody" of said evidence from the very beginning all the way to and through the criminal justice system and the formal closing of the case. Of course, the Evidence Control Unit must meet any and all challenges posed by the defense.

3

Suggested Checklist for the Investigation of Patient Abuse and Neglect

Early on in the growth and development of our investigative skills relating to the criminal acts of patient abuse and neglect, we knew that we would have to create various forms to assist in our efforts. As time went on however, and as we were invited to more and became public speaking engagements and training programs with others in the "loop," it became very clear that we needed relevant and beneficial "handouts." We will cover the contents and investigative benefits of one of these training handouts in this chapter. It is one of the more successful "forms" we ever developed. You will see others as we continue that were and still are beneficial. The first one we will discuss is the basic "building block" form. It is beneficial to all those in the "loop" even including the "providers," meaning Long Term Care Facilities (LTCF), or nursing homes, and group homes for the developmentally disabled adults or other provider settings. It is also important to note here some jurisdictions, such as Maryland, the patient abuse and neglect criminal cite also protects those vulnerable adults not in nursing homes or other settings but in their private homes as they are provided "care" by their families or extended families. In Maryland, one can be charged with the crime of patient abuse and neglect of vulnerable adults, who are under their care or supervision, residing in private homes. These care settings provide a difficult problem for detection by regulatory and law enforcement alike, not dissimilar to the crime of "Child Abuse" occurring in private homes. These settings, which are not the theme of this particular book, are in my opinion, a "hidden iceberg" of patient abuse and neglect in this country.

Simply put, the "Suggested Patient Abuse and Neglect Investigation Checklist," or "Checklist" for short, provides those responsible for the initial investigation or inquiry with an "outline." It has also been described as a "step-by-step" procedures form. Whatever it has been called over the years, I call it "successful" and informative. Our primary intent for the form was that it be provided during "In-Service Training" to supervisory level medical and nursing staff. We designed the form so, if filled out correctly and fully, it would provide the Patient Abuse Coordinator—Unit, with information to access and evaluate a "referral" alleging patient abuse and or neglect. Please remember, we were not in the mandatory reporting "loop" under Maryland law and needed to get the word out there that we "wanted" to be "unofficially" included. This form, once it was circulated via training as handouts or via facsimile to all those in the "loop" did what it was designed to do and much more.

After numerous training and cross-training, the time came wherein our office was receiving completed "Checklists" from not only other government agencies but even the providers themselves! The "Checklist" form became a regular in-coming mail to our office, and from all over the State of Maryland. In time, the "Checklist" forms would come in with additional reports and forms attached. These would normally include police reports, written statements, relevant employee records, "Incident Reports," and staffing records, etc. All this without a subpoena! When completed accurately the "Checklist" provided me with a basic report, which then enabled me to evaluate the alleged incident, enter the allegation(s) into our formal computer data base, brief our legal staff and take certain preliminary investigatory steps. Some of these preliminary steps included calling the facility and asking for additional facility records such as Progress Notes both Nurses and Physician, etc. We will address some examples of medical records and other facility records utilized in the investigation and later criminal prosecution of patient abuse and neglect cases in Chapter Five.

The "Checklist" provides information on the who, what, where, when, how and at times, why, of the reported alleged incidents of abuse and neglect. As part of this chapter you will complete an example "Checklist." Please note many of the entries will seem very elementary, but you would surprised how many times we received written referrals that did not provide such items as the date and time the alleged incident occurred, not to mention the names of the victim and suspect!

Suggested Patient Abuse and Neglect Investigation Checklist Form

Date of incident: 00/00/00

Time of incident: This can assist investigators in establishing a time frame during which the alleged incident(s) occurred, and thus establish witness and possible suspect lists.

Time first reported: This is also important in order to establish if any "late reporting" of the alleged incident(s) occurred.

Person first reporting/discovering injury or condition: Self-explanatory, but this would be helpful in a variety of ways such as determining which staff "found" injuries of unknown origin. Of course, all of the above entries assist investigators in establishing timelines and, thus, narrowing down a possible suspect.

Floor/Wing Room number of the victim: Self-Explanatory and for the record.

Name, age, DOB, of the VICTIM: This is paramount. We must know who our alleged victims are! In the early days, we would at times receive copies of our "Checklists" with this portion of the form intentionally left blank or "blackened" in. Training and cross-training took care of this issue.

VICTIM: Primary Diagnosis, Minimum Data Sheet (MDS): This information includes medical information that enables investigators to have, if you will, a "medical picture" of the victim. The "key" element of the crime of patient abuse and neglect (Maryland's cite) is that the victim be a "vulnerable adult." Medical or mental infirmities establish the fact that the victims are indeed "vulnerable adults." As for the MDS referred to here, in a later chapter we will address specific medical and facility records often gathered and used in the investigation and prosecution of these cases. The MDS is one of them. This form provides detailed information on the patient in total (e.g., full name, DOB, diagnoses, family or responsible party information). The MDS is a brief medical and personal profile of the reported victim. Some examples of information critical to investigators are whether the victim is verbal, mobile, deaf, and whether the victim can be a reliable witness for him/herself.

Injury sustained to the victim?: Yes:_____ No:_____

Injuries of unknown origin?: Yes: ___ No:_____

Photographs taken: Yes:____ No:_____
Note: ALWAYS take photographs!
If yes by whom: Also please provide the date and time the photographs were taken.

Attending physician and phone number: Self-explanatory

Roommates of the victim? If so, name them and primary diagnosis: Some investigators "write off" the possibility that the victim's roommates could also be reliable witnesses. While roommate witnesses are infrequent, roommates can and have been reliable witnesses to alleged patient abuse and neglect. However, when we received information that the "roommates" had been diagnosed with various forms of dementia and/or Alzheimer's, we knew the chances of a roommate witness were greatly diminished. Regardless, it was always beneficial to have the names of roommates "for the record," if nothing else. If there were no roommates to the victim, then this entry can be marked "N/A."

Responsible Party/Family: (Phone numbers):
(Note: Complete information is available on the Admission Sheet.)

List of staff working at the time of the incident: (Assignment Sheets of the Wing/Floor, etc.) Please include the title: CNA, Orderly, LPN, RN, etc. Why would an investigative body want this information? The primary reason is to locate and identify any witnesses and possibly a suspect or suspects. All the individuals listed must have complete and accurate information. If the individual is a CNA (Certified Nurses Assistant), then they must be identified as such. If they are a RN (Registered Nurse), the same applies. Correct titles help the investigator prepare, prioritize and schedule interviews. Also, when asking for home addresses, and home phone numbers, etc. the investigator means exactly that! I can't tell you how many times I asked the facility for all the identifiers on the suspect to include full name, DOB, Social Security number, and home address, only to have the suspect's "home address" listed as the nursing home from which he/she was just terminated for suspected patient abuse and neglect! Why is having the names and identities of other staff in addition to the caregiver assigned to the victim paramount? One reason is to conduct a fair and thorough investigation. Another reason is that it is not uncommon to have incoherent patients abused by other than their "assigned caregiver." You may also recall that over the years I had suspects ranging from doctors, and nurses to visitors and even volunteers. Having complete and accurate information on staff will save precious investigative time and resources when tracking down staff for formal interviews once they are "outside" of the facility.

SUSPECT: Full name, Title, DOB, Social Security Number, home address and phone #: In short, all the information from the personnel file which will enable follow-up investigators to locate suspects outside of the facility. Again, the address of the suspect is not the facility, especially when upon the arrival of even first responders such as law enforcement the suspects have been at least suspended or terminated and long gone. Just an FYI: Unless my interview or interrogation of the suspect was scheduled through their attorney, in all my years as the PAC, I never scheduled an interview appointment with the suspects. Why? I would have lost the element of surprise. Also, the suspects would most likely fail to keep the appointment anyway.

If the SUSPECT is an "agency" or "temporary" employee, please provide the name of the agency and the phone number. Why? As we previously stated, "agency" staff are usually what I have called "phantom caregivers'" coming and going from facility to facility and shift to shift. This portion of the "Checklist" must provide accurate and complete information on the agency that employed the suspect. Merely stating the "name" of the agency is not enough. All facility HR (Human Resources) have POC (Points of Contact) at the various "agency" employers. Providing this information can save the PAC investigator time and precious resources. Of course, if the suspect caregiver was not an "agency" or "temporary" staff than this entry should be marked "N/A."

List the date and time the agency was notified and name the person notified: This establishes the date and time the suspect's employer was notified of the allegation(s) of patient abuse and neglect. At this phase in a preliminary investigation, this is more "for the record" than anything else.

WITNESSES: The full name, Title, Social Security Numbers, DOB, address and phone numbers: All the information requested in this entry is routine, valid, and necessary for any preliminary investigation. The information will enable follow-up investigative staff to locate employee witnesses OUTSIDE of the facility. Another FYI, there were times when I did not schedule interviews of witness staff with the witnesses. Specifically, I would call ahead and make arrangements in confidence with the DN (Director of Nursing), and actually "schedule" the witness interview. Why? I learned the hard way after setting up appointments with the witnesses while they were working, only to come to the appointment and find the witness had suddenly become ill and called off "sick" This was especially a problem or pattern when there was only one known eye witness. Experience over the years revealed that first line caregivers had a pattern of failing to report allegations of patient abuse and neglect, which is both a criminal and regulatory violation. Why? peer pressure or the "veil of silence" code.

WHAT OUTSIDE AGENCIES HAVE BEEN NOTIFIED AND WHEN:
Entries are self-explanatory and for the record, especially since Maryland has a mandatory reporting regulation which clearly outlines the responsibilities of those in the "reporting loop," so often referred to in this book. Of course, as we have documented in this book the Office of the Attorney General Maryland (Medicaid Fraud Control Unit) was not in the "reporting loop" by State regulation but over the years became by way of outreach, reputation and cooperation. Thus, you will find the last agency listed as being "notified" is the Office of the Attorney General, Medicaid Fraud Control Unit, Patient Abuse Unit (PAC). Again, having these entries filled out accurately by the agency forwarding the form to the PAC provides the unit with the bigger picture and of course, it was for the record. It also saves precious investigative time.

Police notified: Date: _____ Time: _____ Report #_____

DHMH—OHCQ: Date: _____ Time: _____ Name: _____
FYI
(DHMH—Maryland's State Health Department formal name is the Department of Health & Mental Hygiene. "OHCQ" The Office of Health Care Quality is the regulatory investigatory agency located within the Department of Health & Mental Hygiene.)

LTCO: Date: _____ Time_____ Name: _____
LTCO is the Long Term Care Ombudsman Office. In Maryland, this office is located within the State Department on Aging. The LTCO has investigative authority and responsibilities under Federal law. There are also local LTCO offices.

OFFICE OF THE ATTORNEY GENERAL
MEDICAID FRAUD CONTROL UNIT
PATIENT ABUSE UNIT: Date: _____ Time: _____

Name: _____
Self-explanatory: This is the person to whom the agency forwarded the "Checklist."

Name and title of the person completing this Checklist: Also include a phone number. Again self-explanatory, but this entry provides the PAC with the name, and by asking for the "title," the qualifications of the person completing the form. The entry can establish a point of contact (POC) for the Office of the Attorney General.

Date Checklist was completed: Self-explanatory, but very informative to the investigator.

CHECKLIST SUMMARY

This form, which was first developed in the mid-1990s has evolved over the years and when completed accurately and completely is a rock solid building block in the investigation of patient abuse and neglect allegations. In time, it was utilized by all those agencies in the "loop," including the nursing homes or other providers of care. As the years proceeded the forms became more refined and thorough and arrived at the Office of the Attorney General—PAC **unsolicited** or simply as a matter of routine correspondence. Also, in time and in conjunction with the arrivals of the "Checklist," our office would also receive copies of the Incident Report (The Internal Investigation of the allegation), photographs and written statements, etc. If your outreach and cross-training works, you will also eventually receive "Checklists" or referrals daily and from all the agencies in the mandatory reporting loop.

4

Suggestions on What to Inform the Police

As we have previously discussed, law enforcement personnel are key to the "foundation" of the patient abuse and neglect criminal investigation. A good foundation will assist follow/up criminal investigators in the completion of the "finished product." However, if the "foundation" lacks the very basic "cement" of facts, then building upon it will be problematic at best. Before we proceed I'm compelled to remind the readers that, like the Marines, once a police officer always a police officer, no matter what your rank or office. This applies to this writer on both counts. However, that said, law enforcement has come a long way since the early days of the patient abuse and neglect laws. However, law enforcement must still continue to improve. Some agencies have established specialized investigative units similar to "Child Abuse Units" to address these crimes at a local level. I can tell you that Maryland's Office of the Attorney General not only supported this concept, but provided training to detectives and investigators assigned to these cases. Some jurisdictions we trained included the Baltimore City State's Attorney's Office, Baltimore County and Baltimore City Police Departments and the West Virginia Office of the Attorney General. We also contributed to a national effort when I attended the Certified Instructor's Course at the Federal Law Enforcement Training Center, Glynco, GA. My certification continues today. This level provided the opportunity to present training to law enforcement personnel from the entire United States.

The **"Suggestions on what to inform the Police"** form was first designed to provide law enforcement some education and insight into the allegations of patient abuse and neglect. However, in time, we utilized it in the education and awareness training of all those in the "loop." Why? After a time, they all started asking for it as a handout in their training and to then pass them out when conducting in-house training or as they refer to it in the nursing home world, "In-

Service Training." We provided training at these sessions year round and throughout the State. You may recall the importance of establishing and maintaining professional rapport with others in the "loop." Being involved in the In-Service Training of personnel working in the facilities caring for vulnerable adults is another example. Again, I will provide the reader with an example of this form with inserts as to why the particular entry is important.

Investigative Suggestions
Patient Abuse and Neglect Investigations (Law Enforcement Personnel)

Obtain a copy of the Internal Investigation/Incident Report

This will provide the first responders, the police, with the "who, what, where, when and why" of the alleged incident. Incident Reports are the critical "building blocks" we addressed earlier.

Obtain any and all written statements submitted by the suspect(s) and witnesses. Written statements can not be emphasized enough. The prosecutors will be interested in written statements, especially those of the suspect. An example of the benefit of written statements would be the detection of any prior statements by the suspect that may be "inconsistent" to the written statement, ("Prior Inconsistent Statements") We will provide some insight to the reader regarding the proper manner for a supervisor to obtain written statements from staff as part of their Internal Report or Incident Report.

Obtain a listing of employees and correct titles. This is all but self-explanatory. The listing with correct titles of employees will assist follow-up investigators with a list of possible witnesses and perhaps, if unknown at the time of the Incident Report, a possible target or suspect for the alleged patient abuse and neglect.

The DN or DON—Director of Nursing should be able to assist you in your investigation and furnish most of the information from the medical chart/record of the victim. Included but not limited to the MDS, and family information, etc. The Director of Nursing is often the ultimate supervisor of medical staff who may be suspects and thus able to provide information regarding the suspect's past performance, present home address and telephone numbers, and all identifiers such as DOB, etc. **The DN is your key point of contact in the facility. This entry provides information to the police as to the point of contact in the**

facility and examples of information that point of contact can access and provide to the investigator. Some staff or employees and even witnesses may be "Agency" or "Temporary" and not actually employed by the facility, thus, the DN will have only very brief information on the "Agency" or "Temporary" medical staff who are suspects or witness. The investigator must then obtain the full name, address and telephone number for the agency employing the suspect or possible witnesses. This entry provides some education to the police that not all "employees" are actually "employed" by the facility and that they must obtain information on just how to contact them by and through other means. Most responses by the facility in which the suspect was working at the time of the alleged patient abuse and neglect are to notify the agency that their employee is not allowed back on their property.

If possible, ask for copies of and review Nurses/Physicians Notes pertaining to the alleged incident. These notes are official and for the record. They will provide follow up investigators with the medical observations of conditions or injuries relative to the alleged incident. As an example, say a "black eye" is observed to have been sustained by an incoherent victim. These notes should provide information on "who" first found the injury, and whom they notified. These notes should provide medical information on "what" the injury or condition looked like to medical staff and when they provided proper medical response to the injury or condition.

Always meet with the victim, unless a doctor or other supervisory medical staff orders otherwise. Give the victim this courtesy. It will also provide you with the opportunity of documenting the appearance or condition of the victim at that time and for the record. Know as much about the victim as possible before you attempt an interview of the victim. Is the victim demented, deaf, blind, etc.? Later in this book we will address techniques for interviewing special witnesses such as victims of Long Term Care Facilities or nursing homes.

Always ... Always take photographs of the victim's injury or conditions and also describe them in your report.

Law enforcement cannot and should not depend on anyone else taking photographs of the injury or conditions of the victim, so they must be prepared to take photographs themselves. I can't emphasize the absolute importance of taking photographs. Progress Notes will be part of any evidence chain for prosecution, but they can't replace the effect photographs have on the jury, not to mention the defense attorney. You know the drill. "A picture is worth a thousand words." It also certainly applies here!

Don't rule out roommates as possible witnesses. Also as part of the investigative record, obtain their MDS, etc. We know what the MDS is right? It is the Minimum Data Sheet which must be maintained and updated on every patient of a nursing home. (Self-explanatory)

Attempt to interview the suspect. Why? Timing in these cases is everything. As I have said over the years, these cases don't age like fine wine. Also, once the suspect leaves the facility because of suspension or termination, they go out into the community and are very difficult to notify let alone be subjected to a formal interview. (Self-explanatory)

OUTSIDE AGENCIES

Office of Health Care Quality, (OHCQ), Maryland's State Health Department also known as the Department of Health & Mental Hygiene (DHMH). This unit monitors and inspects nursing homes and other facilities caring for vulnerable adults. It also has a dedicated unit that investigates allegations of abuse or neglect and other forms of poor care for possible administrative adjudications. Normally, this unit refers "criminal" cases to the Office of the Attorney General, Medicaid Fraud Control Unit and thus, to the PAC.

Long Term Care Ombudsman(LTCO): The Ombudsman operates under the State Department on Aging and has authority, based on Federal Regulations, to investigate allegations of patient abuse and neglect in all its forms, Physical, Sexual, Neglect and Financial, etc. The Long Term Care Ombudsman advocate for patients and their families and are a proven asset to follow-up investigators. Please also note that other sub-divisions in the State of Maryland have phone contact numbers for the "local" office of the Long Term Care Ombudsman.

Office of the Attorney General (OAG)—Medicaid Fraud Control Unit (MFCU) Patient Abuse Unit. Since 1989, the OAG has had a dedicated statewide effort to investigate and, when appropriate, prosecute allegations of criminal patient abuse and neglect, and has successfully prosecuted or adjudicated many, many cases.

This list of "Outside Agencies" is provided as a resource to the police on the identity of others in the "loop" and a brief description of their respective responsibilities. It also informs the "first responders," the police, that their reports go to many places and to many dedicated people. In summary, it provides the police with the "Big Picture."

5

Key Facility Personnel and Records

As an investigator of allegations of patient abuse and neglect you must know some basic key personnel as well as records relative to your investigation. Knowing and being familiar with key personnel and records enables you not only to feel more comfortable operating within the facility, but most importantly, to gather records which will result in a more detailed and in depth investigation. What is your goal? If you are a criminal investigator, your mission is to conduct fair and detailed investigations to ascertain if there is "probable cause" to believe that a crime has been committed. If you are a regulatory agency investigator, your mission is to conduct fair and detailed investigations to ascertain if formal administrative adjudication or other remedies are appropriate. An added responsibility of the regulatory agency investigator is to refer possible criminal cases to the appropriate criminal prosecutorial agency.

The Administrator: This individual is responsible for the entire facility. The he/she is responsible for budgeting, and ensuring the facility meets Medicaid, Medicare and other Federal program and regulatory mandates. The Administrator also meets with outside regulatory agencies and is the supervisor of all personnel both medical and administrative. The Administrator must hold an individual license. When the DN is not available I suggest you ask to meet with or speak with over the phone the Assistant DN or the Administrator. The Administrator can make things happen.

The Director of Nursing (DN or DON): As we have previously discussed the DN, in my opinion, is the "key" point of contact for investigators. My opinion is based on thousands of preliminary investigations, over 300 open case investigations, 88 successful criminal trails or other forms of official adjudications and countless appearances under oath before the Grand Jury and in courts of law. The DN is the ultimate supervisor of all medical staff, other than, of course, the doctors and other outside specialists. The DN is the supervisor of all the caregiver staff, such as Registered Nurses, Licensed Practical Nurses, Certified Nursing Assistants, Certified Medicine Aids, etc. Some of these "titles" may vary from facility and state to state. The DN is the supervisor and often the "hiring authority" for such staff.

The DN is often the designated "Custodian of Records" for the facility. This is extremely important since the investigator will need access to and later obtain copies of relevant facility records, such as assignment sheets, MDS, various Chart Records, such as Physicians and Nursing Notes, etc. It was a very rare event indeed for our office to obtain such records with a subpoena. After establishing our professional rapport, and also with the backing of Federal Regulations, which mandated that the Medicaid Fraud Control Unit have "reasonable access" to such records, we rarely had to subpoena facility records for our investigations. Later, when we approached trial, it was common for our prosecutors to proceed with "copies" and not originals. At times, we would ask the DN to be in possession of "original" facility records at trial. However, you should have the **originals** of any and all written statements, especially those of the suspects. You may recall that I said this book would not be a book about statistics and graphs. It is also not meant to be a "law book." While your writer spent over 35 years working for and around legal staff, he is not an attorney.

The final importance of having a professional rapport with Directors of Nursing comes at trial. Our prosecutors often called Directors of Nursing as expert witnesses at criminal trials. Regulatory agencies can also utilize the expertise of the Director of Nursing at Administrative Hearings. Directors of Nursing can testify as to the medical level of care the victim requires, staffing, performance, and training issues. As a case example, among the first records we look for pertaining to the suspect, after the "Application for Employment," are training records and sign off documents completed by the suspect. If the suspect signed off on the correct methods of providing care (Care Plan) to the reported victim and, during some type of signed off on care, an incident occurred, then the Director of Nursing can testify as to the training provided and that yes indeed the suspect attended and signed off on such training. In one case, which we have already discussed, a Nursing Assistant having previously signed off on training and Care Plan documents on her patient of two years, still left the mentally and physically impaired vulnerable adult in a tub alone while it was still filling with water. Tragically, later the victim was found by another employee, under the water of the over-flowing tub. This incident would not have occurred if the caregiver had followed the Care Plan, which clearly documented that under no circumstances should the patient have been left alone unsupervised in the tub.

I will provide more examples of both knowledge of the Care Plan and the benefit of having the Director of Nursing testify in court. In another case, again involving personal care, a Certified Nursing Assistant violated the patient's Care Plan by "forcing" a male patient under her care into a shower room. The patient had Alzheimer's and his Care Plan, which had been signed off on by the suspect caregiver, clearly documented that under no circumstances should the patient be provided personal care, such as a bath or shower by a female caregiver. The Care Plan documented that this type of care should be provided by male caregivers only. While the patient was being forced into shower, by the female caregiver, the female caregiver assaulted the patient causing head and upper body injuries.

As time went on and as we dealt with more and more facilities and, thus, more and more Directors of Nursing, it was the norm for me to receive completed copies of our "Checklist" and other forms along with the Incident Report or Internal Investigation, and medical and personnel records from the facility in the mail. Often we would receive copies of medical records and training records, etc. unsolicited.

Other Medical staff: At times, it is necessary to call doctor and nurse specialists to trial. Such specialists include nutritional specialists and wound care specialist nurses. This specialized staff is paramount in any criminal case alleging neglect as pertaining to pressure sores, since the treatment requires specialists in this discipline. Often poor nutrition plays a terrible role in the cause and worsening stages of the pressure sores in question. Thus, one can see the need for a nutrition specialist in both the prevention and treatment of pressure sores. We will address pressure sores/bedsores later in this book. Licensed Practical Nurses (LPN) often supervise the frontline caregivers, the Certified Nursing Assistants, and thus, are in a position to provide information pertaining to their observations of the performance of the suspect caregiver. The LPN along with Registered Nurses, can and have been "suspects" as well as "defendants" in the allegations of patient abuse and neglect. Certified Nursing Assistants are the caregiving "backbone" of any LTCF or nursing home. They are in the "trenches" so to speak, as well as the statistical leaders as suspects/defendants. That is not to say that there are plenty of caring and even loving caregivers out there.

However, even caring and loving caregivers can and have been suspects and defendants. In one particular case and another example of "real cases and real faces," our office investigated and successfully prosecuted an award-winning and beloved LPN caregiver employed in a nursing home. When the Administrator called me directly, he was all but in tears as he explained the incident over the phone. In this case it was a male LPN. You may recall my quote that, "Patient abuse and neglect can happen in any facility and at any time." This case is another true case example. It was on a busy AM care morning with breakfast trays coming and going and patients being transferred from bed to other modes such as "Geri-chairs", which are recliners on wheels and one of the most utilized durable medical equipment (DME), in a nursing home. The incident occurred as two female Certified Nursing Assistants CNA, were conducting a routine transfer of a patient who was medically and mentally (Alzheimer's) infirmed. The demented patient, who also had only one leg, was resisting the transfer, and the two CNA staff did the right thing, they called for assistance. Now enters the award-winning, male LPN. As the male LPN attempted to assist he became involved in a physical altercation with the male demented and elderly patient. Before it was over, the two CNA staff were screaming as they watched the male LPN deliver repeated closed fist blows to the head and face of the victim. In fact, the patient abuse ended with the Director of Nursing actually pulling the male LPN off the patient who was now flat on his back with the LPN over him. The male LPN admitted his wrongdoing and was later successfully prosecuted by our office. This case provides the reader with yet another example of "any time and any facility."

Other employees who are non-medical staff: Don't forget other staff of the facility who are not "caregivers." Specifically, I speak about Housekeeping and Maintenance personnel. Why? As a normal course of business they all over the facility and at various times of day. They are also, at times, almost invisible as they quietly go about their duties and tasks. Some are of the opinion that even when they witness a possible patient abuse and neglect, it is not their department and thus, so to speak, not their business. I was told this directly! There were times when we found and later utilized such staffing in our cases. This is why all staff should be trained when you conduct "In-service Training" at the facilities.

The Internal Report/Incident Report: As we have discussed, the Internal Report or Incident Report, at times known as the IR, can be very informative to an investigator. If completed properly and submitted in conjunction with the suggested investigative "Checklist," much of the, who, what, where, when and why, relative to the alleged incident can be answered early on in the preliminary investigation phase. I conducted thousands of "preliminary investigations" that, although necessary at that level, established that I could not proceed to the next. Each facility has an individual "Internal Report" or "Incident Report." Incident Reports are used to document many types of "incidents" occurring in a facility including injuries of unknown origin, patient to patient altercations, missing or lost property, medication errors or missing medications and allegations of patient abuse and neglect. While each facility, which often operates under the corporate umbrella of a large "chain" of nursing homes or other types of providers, has a distinct and respective format, the Incident Reports or IR have taken on certain uniformity. Some of this uniformity, in the State of Maryland at least, I believe can be attributed to the positive effects of the Office of the Attorney General, Medicaid Fraud Control Unit PAC. As we have discussed previously, in time, and after numerous training and cross training sessions, it became the "norm" for our office to receive more and more referrals with more and more information included in the IR, and with attachments enclosed such as the MDS, Progress Notes, written statements from staff, etc. At times I received the Incident Reports before the Police Reports! As a result, I could conduct a very thorough preliminary investigation in a short period of time, and all without subpoenas. **Remember, these cases "don't age like fine wine."**

"Suggested Checklist": Hopefully, the facility has on file a copy of the "Suggested Checklist" and has utilized it during the Internal Investigation. If the facility is not aware of the "Checklist." make them aware. However, it is a "suggested" form and the facility may chose to use it, not use it, or present the information in whatever form they produce. What is important is that timely and accurate information be gathered during the Internal Investigation phase so follow up investigators can proceed.

The Minimum Data Sheet (MDS) on the patient/victim: The Minimum Data Sheet (MDS) is, in short, a medical and personal profile of the patient because it provides not only medical information but family, such as next of kin and the responsible party information on the patient. By Federal regulations, the MDS must be updated periodically and/or when there are any significant changes in the medical condition of the patient. Why is this document important to the criminal investigator? It is important because of all the information we have just discussed. The follow-up investigator and his prosecutor must establish baseline medical information on the patient. Follow-up investigators must at some point contact the family, next of kin and/or responsible party to inform them about the official investigation and to request them appear at or even testify at the trial.

The Admission Sheet: This form documents what the title implies. This document describes the medical conditions of the patient upon being admitted into the facility. It can be of significant importance in any investigation but of paramount importance in cases investigating the possible criminal "neglect" of a patient. Was the patient under weight upon admission? Did the patient have any pressure sores upon admission, and if so what stage?

Suspect employment records: Specifically, the Application for Employment. These records are absolutely necessary to any investigation and even more important at trial. Why? A significant number of "applicants" seem to forget or not to recall certain periods of their employment and education history. Basically, some staff lie providing information or exclude some events while embellishing others. Often there are what I call "broken bridges" in employment histories. We can all be "between jobs" in our lives, but when the broken bridge is because of termination for suspected patient abuse and neglect it is a "home run" for a prosecutor. If this becomes admissible in Court, it can be very damaging to the defense. Private sector employers will tell you that too often they don't have the personnel or time to verify every entry on an Application for Employment and thus at times applicants "slip between the cracks." This fact can cause the facility "big trouble" later.

Suspect training records: As we have previously discussed In-Service records can be a bonanza at trial for a good prosecutor. Participants must not only attend formal training sessions but sign off on the training and Care Plans. The benefit in having these records is almost self-explanatory as we have already provided some examples. Other examples would include the Certificate of training as a Certified Nursing Assistant (CNA), Certified Medicine Assistant (CMA), or Licensed Practical Nurse (LPN).

Communications to the suspect from the facility and regulatory agencies following allegations of patient abuse and neglect. Such as the Board of Nursing, etc. Specifically, letters to the suspect caregiver notifying him/her that the investigation has been initiated, that the suspect's employment status during the investigation has been suspended or terminated. Once terminated, the facility also often orders that the suspect not return to the facility property and if so she/he will be considered trespassing.

Patient-victim Chart and Care Plan: First of all, at least in the State of Maryland, the victim must be established to be, in fact, a "vulnerable adult." In Maryland a "vulnerable adult" is a person 18 and over who has become medically and/or mentally impaired or infirmed. To establish this to the Court the State must produce medical records documenting the respective injuries and/or conditions that describe the victim is indeed a "vulnerable adult." Thus, enters the patient's Chart and Care Plan. These records paint a detailed medical picture, if you will, of the patient-victim. These records document the care level and staff required to provide proper care. It can answer such questions as, does the victim have Alzheimer's, Dementia, limited mobility or no mobility at all? Does the victim have any pressure sores, and if so, what level and what medical care has been provided by the facility? Can the victim be a reliable witness for himself/herself? Can the victim undergo the rigors of appearing at trial and actually taking the stand and testifying against the defendant? In all the years I dedicated to this effort only one time did the victim actually appear at trial. This one case ended in a "Plea Bargain" with the patient not being required to take the stand. In another case in which it was alleged that three vulnerable adult female patients were sexually abused by a female caregiver, all three were indeed "reliable" witnesses. However, their doctor asked us "At what price justice?" The doctor was concerned that the patients could not undergo the rigors of trial. Needless to say we did not call them to trial, but we were successful in obtaining other forms of evidence and our prosecutor prevailed.

The Care Plan for Developmentally Disabled Vulnerable Adults—The Psychological Evaluation of the victim. This describes the level of mental retardation. These documents present to the investigator and later the prosecutor at trial a "picture" of the victim. These include his/her level of mental retardation and what level of care must be provided by the facility to properly care for these, "forgotten vulnerable adults." Nursing home residents can present physical challenges to caregivers, but developmentally disabled vulnerable adults are often fully grown adults with all the strength of adults but the mental ages of children. These vulnerable adults are subjected to all the forms of patient abuse and neglect such as physical, sexual, emotional and financial abuse of those vulnerable adults in nursing homes or Long Term Care Facilities, (LTCF).

Progress Notes both Nurses and Physicians: These notes are formal and for the record. There are strict policy and procedures as to who can make entries and under what circumstances the notes can be amended such as "Late Entry" protocols. I think we all recall the old nursing procedures standard along the lines of "If it is not entered in the Progress Notes (Chart), then it did not happen." These professional notes represent the official documentation of the care and other developments such as "Incidents" occurring in the facility. For example, they may document an injury of unknown origin, alleged patient abuse and or neglect, weight loss and any and all medical issues and plans of care to the patient. They are very critical in allegations of neglect relative to pressure sores, as they should document the history of the pressure sores and the response of the facility to the various stages of the pressure sores. Thus, they are absolutely necessary not only to the investigator but later on to the prosecutor at trial or administrative hearings, should it be determined to be a "regulatory" matter. For example, should injuries of unknown origin occur, these notes, if accurate will provide investigators with at least the, who, what, where and when, as pertaining to the injuries such as a suddenly appearing black eye, of which there was no previous "Incident Report" filed. These notes give the investigator a "jump start" on the investigation.

Social Worker Notes: These are often overlooked by follow-up investigators. However, in some cases they can be very informative. These records, which by the way, are often the most "legible" I have come across, provide in sight into deeper and even historic issues and events occurring at the time of the patient's admission and prior thereto. These records can provide a "bigger picture" of the patient. As I have often said they were once where we are now and where many of us will be tomorrow.

Skin Charts Pressure Sores: Once a pressure sore develops accurate records must be maintained on the care provided. The records should show when the pressure sores were first found, and what steps were taken to address them keep them from progressing to higher stages. These records are crucial for the investigation and possible prosecution of criminal neglect cases, if it can be proven that the pressure sores were caused by the lack of proper care. Such examples include poor hydration, poor nutrition, lack of proper hygiene and lack of proper positioning and turning. Most medical professionals agree that positioning and turning should occur every two hours. In addition to poor hydration and poor nutrition, "friction" contributes to the development of pressure sores. Records on what was done and not done to address pressure sores are absolutely necessary when proceeding to criminal charges. We will cover pressure sores later in this book. I can tell you that criminal neglect cases of this type are difficult to prosecute. The patient may also have secondary medical conditions which contribute to the worsening of pressure sores. There are also "end stage" of life issues which muddy the waters of any criminal prosecution of these cases. This is not to say that they can't be investigated and prosecuted, because they can.

Medication Sheets—"Meds Sheets": These documents can be crucial to any investigation of alleged patient neglect. Especially, if the State is attempting to prove that one of the contributing factors to the victim's "neglect" was the failure of the facility to properly "medicate" the victim. As you know, these documents are "for the record" and must be filled out properly recording the various dates, times and medications administered to the patient and by whom.

Daily Assignment Sheets: These documents enable supervisors to assign caregivers to specific patients and, thus, establish responsibility for those respectfully assigned. At the caregiver/supervisory stage these documents detail the response of the facility to the both the general needs of a particular wing, but most importantly to the needs and wants (Care Plan) of individual patients. For example, two patients in the same room may have significantly different Care Plan needs. If the facility files an "Incident Report" or conducts an internal investigation, Assignment Sheets are one of the first documents gathered while conducting their internal investigation.

Injuries of Unknown Origin Records/Charts: These records document the rates of these types of incidents. Are there more occurring on one shift? Are they occurring more in one wing or floor? If kept accurately, these records can be a "road map" to the investigator in the search for a particular suspect. In extreme cases they can also be utilized to show how the facility addressed or failed to address the indicators and thus contributed to criminal neglect of the patient subjected to intentional patient abuse (Assault) and neglect. One example would be the failure to report an accidental injury and by doing so subjecting the patient to serious medical complications brought on by the caregiver's failure to report the accidental injury. It is well worth repeating, don't become a criminal just because you had an accident with the patient under your care. Injuries of unknown origin are simply visible injuries such as black eyes, bruising, and lacerations, etc., that are "found" to have been sustained to most often incoherent patients. Injuries of unknown origin can be linked to an intentional act of abuse or an incident that is accidental in nature. Although "Incident Reports" and "Progress Notes" by both nurses and doctors are filed, these incidents are often the result of undetected physical abuse or neglect by caregivers, who, of course, fail to report them. Injuries of unknown origin are "found" by other staff. However, it must be stated that not all injuries of unknown origin are a direct result of intentional criminal acts. They can result from the patient bumping the bed rail and causing a bruise or even an attack by another patient. One thing is mandatory for Best Practices by the Director of Nursing and that is to chart any and all incidents of injuries of unknown origin. This charting can be beneficial to both the facility and to follow-up regulatory and criminal investigators.

Written Statements of the suspect (ORIGINALS ARE BEST): Written statements from the suspect should be gathered during any basic "Internal Report" or "Incident Report." Ideally, the written statement should be obtained as soon as possible after the alleged incident. These written statements can come into play if the case goes to criminal trial, especially if issues such as "prior inconsistent statements" enter the arena of the courtroom. The written statements should be just that, "written." by the suspect. They must be signed and dated by the suspect and have a witness to the writing of the statement. If the "written" statement is written in the hand of another at the request of the suspect, then the statement must document that the statement was indeed written in the hand of "another" and at the request of the suspect. The suspect must then provide their respective signatures. Later in this book, we will cover written statements in more detail.

Written Statements of witnesses (ORIGINALS ARE BEST): Much of the above also applies to gathering written statements from witnesses. Internal investigators must do much more than just give a blank piece of paper to a potential witness. Questions should be asked and answers verified. True case example, as part of an Incident Report conducted in a Baltimore City Maryland LTCF we came across a witness statement much along the lines of, "I don't know anything." The written statement was also unsigned and undated. This was the entire written statement. First of all, one might ask "anything" about what? Again, please understand I will never be a nurse supervisor and don't have their skills, but Incident Reports are critical to the "foundation" we have addressed in this book, and, thus, nurse management must be more formally trained in the gathering of information to be included within the final Incident Report.

A copy of the facility "Policy & Protocols" relative to the prohibition of patient abuse and neglect: This document can be useful at trial and/or at an Administrative Hearing. This document can present to the court or hearing that the facility had specific policies and protocols prohibiting patient abuse and neglect in effect at the time of the alleged patient abuse or neglect. Often times employees, including caregivers, are required to "sign off" acknowledging this document. Once again, a document such as this can be devastating to the defense at trial or administrative hearing when the prosecutor asks the defendant if the employee signature acknowledging that the facility will not tolerate patient abuse and neglect is indeed that of the defendant.

6

Pressure Ulcers/Decubitus Ulcers/ Bedsores

As I have advised earlier your writer is neither an attorney nor a medical professional. The views expressed are based on my 35 year professional career in this arena, and of course, my personal notes, reference materials and formal training.

Pressure Ulcers/Decubitus Ulcers[1] or as they are perhaps best known "Pressure Sores" or "Bedsores," which can be devastating to the patient can also lead to actions taken against the facility at both State and Federal levels.

While we in this discipline use several terms to describe and address these conditions, "pressure sores" seems the most appropriate and accurate. Why? While there are other contributors, such as poor hygiene, incontinence, lack of hydration, and poor nutrition, "pressure" is a major cause. After all, one of the paramount "treatments" or methods used to attempt avoidance of "Decubitus Ulcers or Pressure Sores" is to relieve "pressure" on the affected area. Thus, enters the positioning and turning every two hours, a long standing standard just as appropriate now as it ever.

If it can be proven that the pressure sores were caused by intentional neglect by facility staff, then we are not talking about administrative sanctions, but serious criminal charges. Administrative sanctions are serious enough; in some cases the facility may be required to pay thousands of dollars a day in fines until the issuing authorities feel that the remedies are sufficient. "Criminal Neglect" is an insidious and systemic intentional breakdown of the facility to provide the very basic of patient's needs and wants, such as proper medications, treatments, nutrition, hygiene, hydration and scheduled "positioning and turning' every so many hours as deemed appropriate in the patient's respective Care Plan. Some medical professionals and most government oversight agencies will take positions that all

---

1. Taber's Cyclopedic Medical Dictionary, Edition 20, p. 543 defines Decubitus as: "a lying down," "pressure sore," and "A patient's position in bed."

pressure sores are "avoidable" and, thus, all those that develop no matter the "stage," should result in administrative sanctions and/or in criminal charges. I can tell you this, I have seen many wounds and injuries during my career, but a Stage IV Pressure Sore is a sight one never forgets. It is an experience in organic devastation.

We will briefly discuss the four stages later in this chapter, but suffice to say, these are both physically and mentally devastating to the patient. Pressure sores often develop in the bony prominences of the body such as the hips, toes, heels of the feet, back of the head, and ears. They can also develop in other areas of the body such as the buttocks. In short, if the patient is permitted to remain in the same physical position in bed or a "geri-chair," pressure sores will be the result. Period. They can also be very serious and, in the higher stages and in conjunction with other secondary medical conditions and, even fatal. This is not to say that pressure sores can't be aggressively and successfully treated. Pressure sores can over a period of time and with successful treatments be down-graded to Stage I and even totally "healed." However, Stage II pressure sores can rocket up to Stage IV, often because of the lack of some of the most basic caregiver responsibilities such as proper hygiene, proper hydration, proper nutrition and positioning and turning as outlined in the patient's Care Plan. As for being "unavoidable" your writer is not a medical practitioner, especially not a specialist in the recognition and treatment of all the various stages of pressure sores, however, having been in this professional arena a number of years and having been provided training, the only "unavoidable" pressure sores I have seen have been when the Chart extensively documents them and there are secondary medical conditions. However, in numerous cases proper hygiene, nutrition, positioning and turning can control and, in some cases eliminate pressure sores.

To be direct, when the triggers are controlled, the sores are controlled. I don't mean to overly simplify, but at times it can, in fact, be that "simple." For example: What do you expect to happen to the skin integrity of a patient who lacks any mobility, lacks proper care, is not positioned and turned, or properly hydrated or fed? The answer is very simple and also devastating. Medical experts will tell you that, in some cases, in only a matter of hours the skin integrity will start to breakdown with a Stage I appearing and followed very quickly by Stage II and so on if the lack of proper precautions continues.

If the State can develop "probable cause" that the pressure sores were caused by the intentional "neglect" of proper medical treatment, then the state can file criminal charges for patient neglect. Since pressure sores, in some cases, are systemic in nature, these conditions often don't involve one unfortunate patient but can often involve multiple vulnerable adults. The upper stages of pressure sores can also lead to very serious conditions such as blood poisoning and gangrene.

The four stages of Pressure Ulcers/Decubitus Ulcers/Pressure Sores[2]

A pressure ulcer is localized injury to skin and/or underlying tissue usually over bony prominence, as a result of pressure or pressure in combination with shear and/or friction. A number of contributing factors are also associated with pressure ulcers; the significance of these factors is yet to be elucidated.[3]

Stage I: "Intact skin with non-blanchable redness of a localized area usually over a bony prominence. Darkly pigmented skin may not have visible blanching; its color may differ from the surrounding area."

Stage II: "Partial thickness loss of dermis presenting as a shallow open ulcer with red pink wound bed, without slough, "dead matter or necrosed tissue separated from living tissue or ulceration."[4] May also present as an intact or open/ ruptured serum-filled blister."[5]

Stage III: "Full thickness tissue loss. Subcutaneous fat may be visible but not bone. Tendon or muscle is not exposed. Slough may be present but does not obscure the depth of tissue loss. May include undermining and tunneling"

Stage IV: "Full thickness tissue loss with exposed bone, tendon or muscle. Slough or eschar may be present on some parts of the wound bed. Often include undermining and tunneling."

UNSTAGEABLE

"Full thickness tissue loss in which the base of the ulcer is covered by slough (yellow, tan, gray, green or brown) and/or eschar (tan, brown or black) in the wound bed." **Taber's Cyclopedic Medical Dictionary, Edition 20 defines "eschar" as: "Dead matter that is cast from the surface of the skin, esp. after a burn."**

Not to slight Stage I pressure sores, but criminal prosecutions normally involve the systemic neglect leading to Stage III and Stage IV pressure sores and

---

2.   Contents of the following section are based on the Lesson Plan of Joseph S. Bostwick, (Patient Abuse Coordinator/Lead Investigator Maryland Medicaid Fraud Control Unit—Maryland) and Dave Carman (Chief Investigator Delaware Medicaid fraud Control Unit) Federal Law Enforcement Training Center, Instructors.

3.   National Pressure Ulcer Advisory Panel (NPUAP) Newsletter, Vol.21, Spring 2007.

4.   Taber's Cyclopedic Medical Dictionary, Edition 20, p. 2016.

5.   National Pressure Ulcer Advisory Panel (NPUAP) Newsletter, Vol. 21, Spring 2007.

the serious secondary medical conditions they cause, such as blood poisoning, gangrene, and amputations of limbs, etc. Criminal prosecution often follows when there is evidence that that pressure sores are epidemic and as a result of criminal neglect.

What causes them?

Pressure sores develop not only from "pressure" but also from friction and shearing force. Rarely will a pressure sore develop from just one of these three causes. More often, at least two of the causes and frequently all three will combine to create pressure sores.

Pressure exerts a perpendicular force on the skin. An unavoidable consequence of gravity, it occurs regardless of the patient's position in the bed. **Positioning and turning every two hours can literally take the "pressure" off the area in which the pressure sore is developing.** Doctors and nurses will tell you, positioning and turning patients can work! In a criminal case of "neglect," if the state can prove that the Care Plan mandating positioning and turning of the patient was intentionally not followed, it provides another building block in the foundation of a criminal investigation and later conviction for Patient Neglect or, in more severe cases, Reckless Endangerment and in the worst cases Manslaughter.

Friction acts parallel to the skin. Whenever the patient moves in bed, his/her skin rubs against the resistance surface of the bed sheets, producing friction. Friction also occurs when a patient is dragged across a bed rather than being lifted or without a pull sheet." In this case we see yet another example of staff attempting to save time and move on to the next patient. By not following the Care Plan, the caregiver contributes to the development of pressure sores. Once again, if the Care Plan mandates that the patient be repositioned by "lifting" rather than being "dragged" across hot burning sheets, then a possible criminal neglect case can loom ahead. However, as we stated earlier, rarely does "one" contributor or "trigger" cause pressure sores but systematic and intentional patterns can.

Shearing force combines the effects of both pressure and friction.

Maceration, which is caused by excessive moisture, softens the skin and reduces its resistance. This can occur with excessive perspiration, urinary or fecal incontinence. Once again possible criminal Patient Neglect looms when such "triggers" as above go unchecked by nursing supervisory staff. In short, if a patient suffers from urinary or bowel incontinence it is not his/her fault! Guess what. It is the job of the nursing staff to treat and cure the patient and not contribute to the "triggers." If an investigation into allegations of patient neglect shows that patients were not provided proper hygiene following urinary or bowel incontinence, or simple daily hygiene, neglect has already occurred! It is just a matter as to if it has risen to the level of "criminal prosecution" or referral to a formal an Administrative Hearing.

Some of the evidence we would normally gather during a Criminal Neglect investigation relative to pressure sores

The victim's chart: Is the victim coherent? Does the victim have limited or no mobility? Does the patient have a history of pressure sores? If so, when, where, and at what Stages were the previous pressure sores? A patient with limited or no mobility is at a high risk for developing pressure sores. Does the victim have any secondary medical conditions, such as strokes, and end of life conditions that can contribute to the development of pressure sores?

Photographs: I can't overly express the paramount importance of photographs in any patient abuse and neglect case, but in pressure sore cases the need is absolute! Reading medical descriptions and Progress Notes are devastating enough, but photographs of Stage III and Stage IV pressure sores will absolutely stun a courtroom and jury. Why not! They are horrible and, in too many cases, avoidable. However, over the years nursing facilities have progressed in recognizing the importance of a true "specialist" when it comes to pressure sores. Thus, enters the Nurse Wound Care Specialist. These nurses are critical to the facility. In criminal cases we also call upon them as outside expert witnesses.

Speak with the victim! After you check the victim's chart and learn that, although physically incapacitated, the victim is mentally coherent, give the victim the courtesy of speaking with him/her. Perhaps the victim can shed light on what actual care was provided or not provided as "documented" in the chart. Perhaps the chart shows that the victim was provided such preventative care as proper hygiene, hydration, nutrition, and the basic positioning and turning. However, the patient informs you that some or all of the basic preventative measures were not provided or not provided the amount of times documented in the Chart. Example: The patient may not recall everything that occurs during the overnight and perhaps is not coherent when all the positioning and turning is documented as being provided, but the patient often does recall such positioning and turning, especially if it is painful, and it can be. The patient is also positioned and turned during the daylight hours, or should be. Also, again, what about roommates? If the roommate is coherent perhaps more light could be shed on exactly what particular care was rendered, by whom, and when. Don't build your investigative or criminal case on these building blocks alone, but they can still be part of the finished product.

Positioning and Turning Records: As basic as they sound they are an official record of the caregiver's addressing these pressure sores at the frontlines of basic care. However, have Positioning and Turning records been falsified? At times I did tend to think that such records had false entries.

Any and all records documenting when the pressure sores were first noticed and by whom: How were the observations documented? An example would be, upon admission into the nursing home from another. You can be assured that the Admission Department medical staff look for and document pressure sores that pre-date the admission.

Any and all documentation on treatments rendered to the pressure sores. The length of time the patient has been in the nursing home.

If the patient was admitted into the facility with pressure sores and the patient was admitted from another nursing facility, follow the paper trail. Obtain the records from the previous facility to determine if the patient actually had pressure sores and, if so, at what stage. If you walk into the patient's room and observe a Stage III pressure sore and the patient was discharged very recently from the previous facility with an early Stage I pressure sore, then the present facility has some questions to answer.

Just because pressure sores are more a condition than an actual "assault" or physical "attack," does not mean the investigator should not follow the usual investigative course of who, what, where, when and why, etc. So the investigator should still speak with or interview staff at all levels, such as doctors, nurses, and CNAs.

Speaking of caregivers, check the training records of the staff most assigned to the victim. Did they sign off on proper positioning and turning, proper hygiene, hydration and nutrition? Ask questions such as, what are the caregivers instructed to do if, after a patient is positioned and turned, the patient then moves directly back to the previous position? My experience in this field would suggest that the caregivers are instructed to re-position the patient. However, I respectively suggest, that more than not, the caregivers just wait for the next two hour routine. The investigator must obtain any and all facility records demonstrating the proper methods of positioning and turning.

Conduct an interview of the Nurse Wound Care Specialist. This specialist can shed the most light on the treatments provided to the patient and the efforts to avoid pressure sores and/or how proper medical treatment can limit the stages. This specialist will be called upon to testify at trial anyway, so take the opportunity of a "for the record" interview. The expert testimony of the Nurse Wound Care Specialist can educate the court on pressures sores, and also shed light on any inconsistencies found in progress notes entered by other staff. This testimony can be beneficial to the prosecution in establishing for the court that inconsistent statements are documented in the official facility records such as progress notes. If you are fortunate enough to have a Registered Nurse assigned to your Patient Abuse Unit, then request that the RN review the medical documents seized, and most importantly, the Nurse Wound Care Specialist's records of care and treatment.

Remember the most prominent "triggers" for the development of pressure sores are: end of life conditions, other secondary medical conditions, lack of or limited mobility, poor hygiene, lack of proper hydration, and lack of very basics, the proper positioning and turning routine.

These cases can be difficult to investigate and even more difficult to prosecute. However, they can be successfully investigated and prosecuted. These cases take much more investigative and research time due to the extensive medical records that must be reviewed and then augmented by in-depth interviews of staff at all levels, CNA, LPN, DN, Nurse Wound Care Specialist and Physicians. **The investigative road can take you to the previous facility of care to conduct a "mirror" investigation there.** The road to a successful investigation and, if appropriate, prosecution of a pressure sore case is often long and full of obstacles, but worth the travel in pursuit of justice.

This has been but a brief overview of the issues of pressure sores with regards to causes, avoidance, care, and when appropriate, criminal prosecution. For additional information you can access the National Pressure Ulcer Advisory Panel (NPUAP) at www.npuap.org.

7

Suggested Methods of Interviewing Special Witnesses and Elderly Victims

This portion of the book will provide insight on interviewing special witnesses and elderly victims. The information in this chapter is based on my years of conducting interviews and interrogations.

Before interviewing the patient, the investigator should review the case including the patient's Chart, MDS and other relevant records. Following this, the investigator can consider what, if any, information the patient or witness can contribute. I learned this the hard way back in 1989, when I was investigating an alleged patient abuse in a nursing home. Although I had a whole career behind me as a detective sergeant, I was a "new guy" in this arena. I was busy, but that was still no excuse, so I did my usual professional meeting with the DN and asked to be escorted to the victim's room to conduct an interview. I was told that the victim was coherent, but I did not check the Chart or MDS for all the details. I walked into the patient's room and provided her the courtesy of a greeting while displaying my ID and badge. I also gave her my business card. While she seemed to be receptive to me, she did not provide any verbal response. I usually asked for the DN or another Nurse to be in the room during my introduction phase. The Nurse staff would then leave once I started the actual interview. In this case, I looked over to the Nurse with an expression that negated the necessity of verbal exchange. The Nurse then told me that the patient was deaf. Chalk one up to experience!

Plan the interview. Produce a "list" of points to address. At times, although coherent, elderly victims can if I may say, with no disrespect intended, "ramble" on a bit. This can throw the investigator off track and, thus, some points previously sought for during the interview can be lost in the maze of rambling. Also, even if the witness never actually appears at trial, this is not to say the investigator can't obtain some relevant information. Remember, "building blocks," one brick at a time.

As we have addressed, timing is critical in the investigation of a patient abuse and neglect case. Although, in most cases, you can be sure your victim will be in the facility on the date of interview that does not mean smooth sailing. Beware and try not to interfere with the time of day issues such as, time of daily care, and time of day for the individual habits or the Care Plan of the victim. Try not to interfere with the victim's activities of daily living (ADL). If the investigator interrupts some type of special activity the victim looks forward to, then the victim may become agitated. Please understand, many of the most routine activities of daily living we all take for granted can take on a whole new dimension for the patient. Such things as "lunch" can be the most enjoyable part of the patient's day. So now enters this complete stranger, you, flashing a badge and interrupting the patient's pleasure of which I remind you they have very little.

The investigator should control the environment, as best as possible. No distractions. Keep nursing staff and other employees out of the room. Don't conduct what I have called, over the years, "peanut gallery" interviews. Too many staff in the room will, and I guarantee it, cause you problems later. You should also suggest this to Administrative staff of the facility when they initiate the Incident Report or Internal Report. It is often best to have a female investigator with a male investigator as he conducts the interview of a female victim, especially if the allegation is of sexual abuse. If no female investigator is available, perhaps you could call upon the service of the RN assigned to your unit or an RN Nurse Surveyor from your State Health Department. This can be beneficial in several ways. First, it makes the female patient more comfortable dealing with an already stressful and painful incident, and secondly, you reinforce the professional rapport with other agencies that I have stressed so much in this book. Finally, we can all learn from others, so taking along a Nurse Surveyor can both benefit the case and add to your personal investigative skills.

Physical impairments will determine if the victim can or cannot be used as a witness during a formal proceeding such as criminal trials or administrative hearing.

Mental impairments will determine the validity of information obtained. True case example: I had a case involving the alleged physical abuse of a developmentally disabled male. The victim had the mental age of a child less than seven years old. While he could never have undergone the rigors of trial, his interview was very beneficial to our case and its resulting successful prosecution. The incident took place over the weekend at a group home for mentally disabled vulnerable adults. In Maryland, our patient abuse and neglect criminal cite also protects developmentally disabled vulnerable adults. As stated, we could never actually call the victim to testify, however, both in the Incident Report and in our subsequent criminal investigation the victim was consistent in stating that his injuries, which were extensive bruising to both legs and "belt welts" on his buttocks, happened at the stair case; and he then repeated "belt and shoe, belt and shoe." The photographs clearly depicted "belt welts" and the bruising in the shape of the sole of a shoe.

There were only two caregivers assigned to the victim for the entire weekend and the injuries, however, were found by the Monday morning staff, who immediately reported them. Of course, as you can guess, no Incident Report, no Accident Report, or no Unusual Episode Report was filed by the weekend staff. One caregiver spent most of the weekend with the victim. The photographs were huge in the successful prosecution of this case. In summary, don't write-off the great potential for information you can obtain from those vulnerable adult victims who can not present formal testimony in a court of law. Please always keep in mind the "building block" analogy I have addressed in this book.

Developmentally Disabled Adults as witnesses at Trial: A word of caution pertaining to the qualification of developmentally disabled vulnerable adults testifying at trial. Some of the victims in these cases, while clearly developmentally disabled, also have the mental ages of children. At times "children" can qualify to testify in a court of law. This is determined by the court via contributions and opinions from legal and medical experts. However, I can tell you as a practical matter, placing a developmentally disabled adult on the stand can be very risky. These victims are often taking a significant amount of medication to "control" emotional and, even physical "episodes." However, sadly, "episodes" can still occur and on the stand during trial. Can you imagine the positive effect this has on the case for the defense? This never occurred to me or to my prosecutors at trial, although once I was struck by a developmentally disabled patient. However, I did take part in a national training seminar wherein one of the other investigator presenters played a videotape depicting the rather controlled and methodical questioning of a developmentally disabled victim. Suddenly, the court was violently changed as the victim left the stand while screaming uncontrollably. The episode, which seemed almost endless on the videotape, ended only after the victim's female primary caregiver gently "talked and walked" the victim through it. While your heart went out to the developmentally disabled adult victim, one can only describe the caregiver as a "saint." The entire time she was "walking and talking" the victim through his episode, he had hold of her face in a vice-like grip.

The female caregiver repeatedly waved off requests for intervention by others in the courtroom. The videotape had a very profound effect on the professionals attending the training. What was the result of the criminal case? The suspect caregiver, who was accused of sexually abusing the victim, was found guilty!

Knowledge of the victim's personal history assists the investigator in establishing a rapport with a victim. It enables the investigator, as part of what I have always referred to as the "preamble" to the interview, to engage in "conversation" with the victim about such things as his/her family, past profession, etc. In summary, don't walk in cold, flash your badge and abruptly start your interview. It is difficult enough for the victim to relive the nightmare of the patient abuse. "Real cases and real faces" example: We had a case wherein an elderly female patient, also diagnosed with dementia, resided in a nursing home. The female victim had sustained a severe injury to one of her lower legs. The victim had secondary medical conditions which only made the already significant injury worse and she almost lost her lower leg to gangrene. Again, this is another example of the benefits of always personally meeting with the victims no matter what the MDS, or other relevant medical documents reveal. I always do so as a courtesy, at the least. While this female patient was clearly unable to be a reliable witness, I still learned some things from her interview. The incident was reported by her lone caregiver, a female certified nursing assistant (CNA). The CNA suspect reported that the victim was standing by a dresser in her private room, when suddenly and without cause the victim became agitated and kicked "at" the caregiver but missed and struck her lower leg on the edge of the table portion of the over-the-bed table (OBT). Please keep in mind, the suspect advised that the victim's lower leg struck the "edge" of the table portion of the OBT. I'm sure we all know what purpose these devices serve. Well, first of all I followed the suggestions previously provided in this book and gently began my interview, especially, as the elderly, but still very refined female victim welcomed me into her "parlor" (private room), as I was, in her words, her "guest." Before it was over it was clear that this victim could never, and I mean never, have sustained the severe laceration by kicking at the suspect caregiver, missing the suspect and, then striking the edge of the "table" portion of the over-the bed-table. Why? Quite simply the victim lacked the range of motion (ROM) to have kicked and reached high enough off the floor to strike her leg as described. If she had, perhaps the NFL could have drafted her in her youth! We established this by measuring her walking paces and the height of the table portion at its maximum and minimum heights. The math was impossible. After lengthy interrogation, the suspect finally gave up the myth and admitted guilt and our prosecutors prevailed at trial. What really occurred? The suspect intentionally kicked the victim's leg.

Know the medications the victim is taking or was taking at the time of the alleged abuse. Why? Knowledge of this information assists the investigator in determining both the physical and mental factors involved in the alleged patient abuse. Some examples include any history of bruising easily due to medications and periods of delusional behavior, etc. This is not to say that the patient could not still be the victim of patient abuse, but it is vital knowledge to both the investigator and the prosecutor during trial preparations and trial.

The relationship existing between the investigator and the elderly patient will determine the success of the interview. Once again, this is a reminder of the importance of your first encounter with the victim. We all know the drill that we only have one chance to make a first impression. This also applies here. Schedule and build into your interview time for social conversation and don't just jump into "just the facts" role.

Be sincere with the patient. If the timing is correct and your "read" of the patient's body language suggests that a touching or holding of the patient's hand would be appropriate, then do it! Show sincere compassion. It won't hurt the patient or you, I promise. True case example: We had a case involving the alleged sexual assault of a vulnerable adult male patient residing in a very exclusive nursing home in Baltimore, Maryland. Remember; "Patient abuse and neglect can happen in any facility and at any time." The male victim, who was only in his forties, was in the facility due to a progressive bone disease, which actually started in his early childhood. He also had severe speech impediment. He was confined to bed with no mobility at all except for the use of one very small childlike arm and hand to press "letters" on a voice box communicator. His interview would be one of the most difficult and emotional victim interviews I have ever conducted. First, of course, I reviewed his MDS and spoke with staff and learned that the victim had a "nickname" that he actually liked to be called by and that his favorite rock group was the "Rolling Stones." The allegation was that in broad daylight, as he lay asleep in his bed, in a private room, a male "volunteer" caregiver sexually assaulted him. The victim awakened to find the volunteer caregiver kissing him full on the mouth while fondling his genitals. The victim could scream and did so as he bravely fought off his attacker with his one "childlike" arm. My interview took four hours. If I had not shown true compassion it would not have lasted five minutes. This victim was one of the bravest men I have ever known. The only way he could ambulate was via a scooter. Although, our legal staff and the defense had agreed upon a reasonable Plea Bargain, this brave man came to trial to confront his attacker and to stand up for his manhood. When he entered the court-room, a packed Baltimore Court, the room went dead silent. You see, the Judge had already heard the Statement of Facts and the proposed Plea Bargain and had accepted it. The Judge even left the bench to come down and explain the Plea Bargain to the victim. Six months later, the case was completely adjudicated, with no appeal possible. Thus, there was no conflict of interest involved. I received repeated phone calls from the victim "through" the staff at the LTCF, informing me that he wanted to go out to lunch with me and the prosecutor, AAG Cathe-rine Schuster Pascale. We did in fact go to lunch with the victim. The establish-ment was right across the street from the nursing home and the victim often visited there via his scooter. It was a beautiful day and I took photographs for the victim. We placed our orders and the victim ordered a large hamburger with the "works." I mean the works. Well, what a lesson we learned that day. We were all seated and Cathy and I began to eat. What were we thinking! The victim could not perform this activity of daily living. So in a matter of moments, I became his caregiver as I assisted him in eating his lunch. I will never forget this man. Assis-tant Attorney General Catherine Schuster Pascale and I still have the photographs taken that beautiful day, an especially beautiful one for the victim.

Avoid using medial terms or "legal jargon," during the interview.

During the interview allow times for periods of rest for the victim.

The elements of the alleged offense and other points in the case serve as your "guide posts." Don't stray, unless it is for just cause. After the patient has pro-vided his/her account, review it with him/her to determine which points need refinement. **Take your time.**

Control the direction of the interview. Notice, I said direction not the "out-come." Always remember that we seek the truth. Questions should not be asked until the patient appears prepared to give the information in an accurate manner. Remember this is not an interrogation. No rapid fire questions. Avoid long and complicated legalistic questions. Allow time and display patience. Attempt to refine questionable points of relevance. Remember, we can all, at times, become a little confused. The victim can be nervous, and even embarrassed talking to a per-fect stranger about how he/she was violated.

At times, when discrepancies and inaccuracies become apparent during the interview, attempt to refine the information. Again, please remember we seek the facts. We seek truth. It is our duty. If you do discover inaccuracies or discrepan-cies, don't wait until trial to inform the prosecutor!

We seek the truth. Our victims often require special interviewing techniques. The investigator must be prepared to deal with the fact that many of the patients feel loneliness, mistrust, and sometimes indifference towards the investigator and his/her goals. Remember, the world of the victim is often, unfortunately, much different and "smaller' than ours. Specifically, while the patient may have had a wonderful successful personal and professional life, he/she is now in another world. Also remember, especially in alleged repeated attacks, once you enter the facility you have the option of leaving. You often never return for whatever reason, while the patient remains in the "other world." Apathy and depression are real issues to deal with when speaking with patient abuse and neglect victims, who are not dissimilar from victims of child abuse and spousal abuse. When you leave, the patient is right back in the hands of the alleged suspect and is vulnerable. He/she is alone. He/she often never leaves the "other world."

8

General Investigative Procedures for both Internal and Criminal Investigations

I was never challenged in open court or otherwise of, violating the Constitutional Rights of a suspect or defendant, nor should I have been. The point here is that when we proceed in this long chapter with suggestions and techniques of conducting interviews, be they of the suspect or of others, the suggestions are tried and true to me. I only sought the truth which would enable our prosecutors to proceed to criminal trial with the very best case possible from my level. These are suggestions which will be again laced with "real cases and real faces." so to speak, that work for me. You have to do what works for you with the guidance of your legal staff.

In addition, and as stated previously, my lesson plans through years of formal training both locally and nationally also contribute to this book. I had the opportunity of both providing and also receiving excellent training as stated locally and nationally. When we move through this chapter and discuss suggestions on how to conduct Internal Investigations (Incident Reports) by administrations of nursing homes and other facilities of care for vulnerable adults, again, the suggestions are based on what now have become standard operations in many such provider locations in Maryland. Why? This was accomplished by, as I first stated, establishing and maintaining relationships with all those in the reporting "loop." I presented training to the point where I almost had to turn down numerous requests for in-service training at nursing homes, other locations of care, other regulatory government agencies, and finally, law enforcement. However, in the end, because of our extensive out-reach training program, we all reaped the resulting benefits. Our never-ending cycles of training helped established professional rapport. Finally, and most importantly, I had the opportunity of conducting criminal investigations which established probable cause and later successful prosecutions.

Suspect interviews/interrogations at the criminal investigations level

First of all, and for the record, for all the active law enforcement professionals out there, Miranda Rights! I will not insult your intelligence and years of experience to comment much further on this matter. I will say a criminal investigator must know when it is legally necessary to issue the Miranda Warning and the investigator must also follow the legal advice and instructions of his/her legal staff. You will note later on in this chapter, as I lace it with "real cases and real faces" that I rarely issued the Miranda Warning. However, when I did, it was the correct and legal step to take. When I did not it was also the correct and legal step to take. The final point to all those out there in the law enforcement world, when the suspect asks for or obtains an attorney all the rules of "our" Constitutional rights apply. Period.

Preparation for conducting the criminal suspect interview/ interrogation

Once your investigation has started and you have received information from an Incident Report or the Internal Investigation Report and suspect information has been provided or you later develop a suspect on your own, you must prepare for the interview. This is not a "street crime" such as an armed robbery, wherein things can happen lighting fast and furious. In these cases, on most occasions, we have the time to step back and gather extensive information on the suspect and thus, are well prepared for at least an initial interview. Why? In most cases by the time the police arrive to take the initial report of investigation the suspect has been suspended or terminated. Rarely, in the State of Maryland do the local police proceed much past the first responders level for what ever reasons, such as lack of trained personnel to proceed or a relationship of formal referrals to a state level agency such as the Office of the Attorney General, Medicaid Fraud Control Unit-Patient Abuse Unit. Of course, this is a different situation when we have a case of alleged criminal Neglect and we develop a suspect or suspects on our own. It can also occur in other cases, such as in a classic "injuries of unknown origin" case in which we later develop probable cause to believe the injuries were caused by an intentional attack or acts of criminal neglect. Example: A caregiver **accidentally** drops an incoherent patient causing visible injuries or not, but then just places the patient back into bed and fails to report the incident, consequently, denying the patient proper medical assistance and treatment. Later another caregiver finds this same patient in the bed having sustained fractures or some other possibly life threatening conditions. In Maryland, that is probable cause for a

Patient Neglect charge at the least. Another criminal charge that could be appropriate is Reckless Endangerment. To all those law enforcement professionals, some of this information will not be the first time passing through your, as we used to say in the Marine Corps, "brain housing group," but that does not mean that we can't still learn and, thus, better protect those we are sworn to protect and serve.

The nursing homes or other facilities providing care for the victim have most of the information necessary to conduct your initial preparations. As law enforcement officers you have the other tools, such as access to criminal history archives, motor vehicle records, and State vital statistics records, just to name a few. If necessary, of course, you also have through your prosecutor, subpoena powers and possible Grand Jury testimony to gather additional forms of information.

We will now discuss some of the records I suggest you obtain to prepare for your suspect interview. If you have not already obtained a copy of the facility Incident or Internal Investigation report get one prior to the suspect interview. Most of the information you will need is also listed in the "Suggested Checklist" and Chapter Three of this book. Here we will expand on the benefits of obtaining these records and reviewing them prior to your suspect interview, and, if necessary, referring to them during your interview. Example: Say you want to refresh the suspect's memory of the fact that he/she failed to list a nursing home employer in his/her present and past Applications for Employment. During your preparation and review of the suspect's Application for Employment and your follow up work, you determined that the suspect did work at another facility but was terminated for "suspected" patient abuse and neglect, but not formally charged. Of course, the suspect would not exactly want this listed on his Application for Employment, and consequently simply "forgot" to list it. You have already scored the first points against the suspect and later at trial because of the establishment of his/her lack of veracity and credibility.

The paper trail left by the Incident Report and other facility records can be very revealing. Obtain copies of any and all written statements submitted by the suspect and witnesses. **You should have already obtained or at least reviewed the victim's Care Plan so you can "know the victim" before you confront the suspect.** Other records you should have already obtained or at least reviewed are the Assignment Sheets for the "window of opportunity" of the alleged abuse. Why? First of all, just because the "assigned caregiver" is often the first target of the investigation, does not mean that he/she is your "suspect" in the end. The facility is not a prison and caregivers come and go, and are in and out of rooms at all times of day and night. The Assignment Sheets will provide you with the names and titles of other staff that may be nothing to your investigation, your only eyewitness, or the suspect. Run a Criminal Records Check on your suspect and key witnesses both local and national. **You never want your prosecutor standing up in Court and first learning that one of your key witnesses has a criminal record.** Of course, you would definitely want a copy of the initial police report and any and all supplemental reports filed on the police response. Obtain the entire Employment File of the suspect. I would add that if you receive the file of a long-time employee and it's five inches thick, your review and obtaining of records may only cover a specified period of time as appropriate. If in doubt, follow the advice of your legal staff.

The Application for Employment might be ancient history. Regardless, the Employment File of the suspect is a possible bonanza of information critical for your investigation and later prosecution by your supervisory legal staff. Why? This document is well known to contain a myriad of misleading if not out right deceitful information furnished in "the own words" of the suspect. Even the professional providers of care to vulnerable adults have acknowledged the problem of the failure of Human Resources (HR) to more thoroughly check out the Applications for Employment. For example, are there broken periods of employment with without explanations? What I call "broken bridges." Other examples include vague answers and false or embellished educational and training entries. While the applicant must have an up-to-date "certification," false or misleading entries are critical information for your investigation in preparation for your interview and later for the prosecutor. Why? All the misleading and out right false entries can establish a lack of credibility for the suspect both while you conduct the interview and later at trial. A lot of courtroom strategies, such as the introduction into evidence of photographs of the victim's injuries, can have a very profound effect on the jury. Having the defendant take the stand as the prosecutor proceeds to destroy his/her credibility as the prosecutor walks the defendant through his/her own employment file pointing out false entry after false entry is another. A final word on the importance of detailed investigations and verifications of Applications for Employment comes from a September 2006 Baltimore newspaper. The story involved a 24-year old employee of a very large inner city hospital. The employee was charged with numerous counts of "identity theft" of patients in the hospital. Specifically, the defendant is alleged to have pulled patient's records in order to "steal" their Social Security numbers. The point here is the Sun Paper article lists seven "also know as" (AKA), identities for the suspect. Now one has to wonder just what was listed in the defendant's Application for Employment. Good question wouldn't you say?

Within the Employment file you should locate and have available for your attorney copies of any and all of the suspect's training records. Why are these important? We have briefly discussed this, but again these records often have documents with "Sign Offs" by the suspect on relevant documents relating to the victim's Care Plan. Again, why is this important? It is important, for example, if the Care Plan documents that the patient must be positioned and turned, fed a certain diet, hydrated properly and/or provided proper hygiene to avoid pressure sores or limit the increase in their stages. If "Patient Neglect" results you are well on your way to establishing probable cause to believe a crime has been committed. Care Plans are often "signed off" on by the suspect and thus, are critical to your criminal investigation and later at trial. Again, you may recall my example case of the helpless infant-like victim being intentionally left alone and completely unsupervised in a tub later to be found by facility staff drown. The suspect caregiver in this case "signed off" on the victim's Care Plan and had also been assigned to care for the victim for two years. We took the case before the Grand Jury and, after very lengthy testimony, indictments were returned for among other things, Involuntary Manslaughter. Our legal staff, in the form of Alexis Taylor, of the Office of the Inspector General for Washington, DC, Medicaid Fraud Control Unit, later successfully assisted the Federal Prosecutor in the successful adjudication of this case.

Records pertaining to "injuries of unknown origin" can also be critical to your investigation and later at trial. As we previously discussed, injuries of unknown origin can and will happen in any nursing home or other facility in the business of caring for vulnerable adults. However, it is also safe to say that some of these injuries are sustained as a result of an accident occurring during care and simply not reported. They also occur as a direct act of patient abuse and neglect. Specifically, intentional assault and battery attacks. True case example: We had a case wherein the suspect literally walked from nursing home to nursing home in Baltimore City, Maryland, physically abusing elderly and vulnerable male patients. He was suspected of patient abuse in several facilities all during a relatively short period of time. Why? He left a trail of broken patients as he traveled from facility to facility with his recognized and legal certificate as a "Certified Nursing Assistant" in hand. At times, facilities "hired" applicants on the spot due to shortages and before Maryland made it a requirement to run criminal history checks on direct and other caregiver staff. I recall, one of the most respected nursing home administrators in Baltimore City showing me a very tall "stack" of positive Criminal History Checks, which he paid to have run on Certified Nursing Assistant staff and other applicants before Maryland law made such checks mandatory. He was truly ahead of his time and even offered testimony at our General Assembly in favor of passing the law that did in fact make such Criminal History Checks mandatory in Maryland. Why did he keep the "tall stack" of positive criminal history checks on his desk? He told me he did it to remind himself of the benefit of the costs to run the checks as opposed to unknowingly hiring "convicted" felons. Applicants with felony records for such crimes as robbery, assault with the intent to murder, and hand gun violations had applied to work at his facility, and to "care for" vulnerable adults. Maryland's Office of the Attorney General, lead by J. Joseph Curran, Jr., was instrumental in presenting testimony before our State law makers which eventually lead to the passage of a mandatory Criminal History Background Check Law in our State. Assistant Attorney General Timothy U. Sharpe, spearheaded the efforts of the Medicaid Fraud Control Unit in this monumental effort.

Now, lets get back to our "real cases and real faces" example. I tracked this suspect down to another facility after his terminations from other facilities for suspected patient abuse. I first met privately with the Director of Nursing. I asked her a series of questions dealing with "injuries of unknown origin," which are often "charted" by medical staff. I asked her if the facility kept such a chart and she said, yes. I asked her if the facility had experienced an increase in injuries of unknown origin recently, after the hiring of my suspect. She said yes. Now it was becoming very clear to her why I was there. I asked her what I already knew, if the facility had recently hired my suspect. She became alarmed at that point and said, yes. Finally, I asked if the shift the suspect worked experienced a marked increase in injuries of unknown origin? Yes! I then learned that the shift the suspect was assigned was working at that very moment. However, the suspect was off duty.

I took a chance and requested to speak with the suspect's entire shift. As the Director of Nursing went about arranging for staff to report individually to her office, I prepared a list of questions to ask each staff member. Note: The Director of Nursing had been asked not to inform staff what the matter concerned, just to report to her office, which I had set up for my interviews. I must also note that this was an extraordinary case and I don't recommend this step as a "routine" one during your "on-site" investigations. Of course, I don't exclude it. Well, true to her word the DN had staff report to her office "my interview room", one by one and we were alone as I had requested. One by one I proceeded to conduct very brief but targeted interviews of the staff. After providing staff the courtesy of my identification and business card, I conducted the interview. I asked if staff had witnessed any form of patient abuse and neglect, specifically, the intentional physical attacks on patients. After some time of conducting this series of interviews the break came.

I had gone through my standard "preamble" to the interview with a young female caregiver, when she suddenly got up out of her chair went to the closed office door, locked it, and sat back down. Several things went through my mind at the actions of this possible witness. However, the real reason was that the female caregiver was frightened, very frightened of the suspect. They had once had a relationship, but no more. The suspect was violent, very violent. In the end, my witness became our only "eye witness," and furnished the key to our investigation and subsequent successful prosecution of the suspect caregiver. After we successfully prosecuted the defendant, and he was imprisoned, he consented to be interviewed. Of course, for those law enforcement folks out there, you bet, I did provide him his Miranda Warning. In the end, he gave up enough for us to charge him for additional cases of patient abuse. We learned of other cases of the Assault & Battery of other male vulnerable adults. Basically, the suspect could be described as just a thug. If he had a "bad day" at home, beware the patient who needed assistance with personal care such a bowel movement (BM). Why he ever freely agreed to allow me to conduct his interview while he was incarcerated is a true mystery. This is another "real cases and real faces" example for your review. In this case we established the benefit of reviewing and, when necessary, obtaining copies of charts documenting "injuries of unknown origin." We also addressed how, at times, the investigator must be prepared to be flexible while addressing these cases and seeking the truth. It is also an example, which became the "norm" for me over the years by the way, to set up "investigative shop" within the nursing home or other care setting. This comes after successful outreach and maintenance of professional relationships. When I retired, an administrator of a very large corporation of nursing homes attended the affair. When it came time for his individual testimonial, the administrator stated that when he and other administrators dealt with me professionally, they felt that I made them part of the solution, and not part of the problem. His gracious testimonial was also noteworthy, because over the years I also conducted criminal investigations into allegations of criminal neglect alleged to have occurred in nursing homes and other care settings. Specifically, the "targets" of these investigations were both staff and nursing home management.

Other records important in preparation for suspect interviews are those of any and all communications between the suspect and various State regulatory agencies. These agencies will most likely be those providing "licenses" for Doctors, Registered Nurses, and Licensed Practical Nurses, and "certifications" for Certified Nursing Assistants, and Certified Medicine Aides. Why are these records important? These records contain possible relevant information on the suspect regarding any prior complaints and or performance matters. Was the suspect a previous target of a criminal or regulatory investigation? If so, what was the conclusion or finding of fact? Was the suspect exonerated, suspended or terminated as result of any prior allegations? A reminder, the more you know about the suspect of your investigation the stronger your position will be when you sit across the table from, him/her during the interview phase.

Should allegations of "patient neglect" be filed against a nursing home, access to any and all relevant inspection reports by the State Health Department surveyors is paramount. Why? These survey reports are a possible bonanza of information that might be relevant to the investigation of alleged patient neglect. Was the facility previously cited by the regulatory agency for allegations of patient neglect? Was the facility a target of a previous criminal probe for alleged neglect by another law enforcement agency? If so, what were the findings of fact? One obvious example would be in the case of a need to correct violations of care regarding the development and stages of pressure sores. What was the finding of fact? What was the "Plan for Correction" filed by the facility and was it successful? If your investigation follows shortly after a successful "Plan of Correction" relative to pressure sores was submitted by the facility and yet an epidemic of pressure sores has occurred, this is pertinent information for your present case.

All of the above-mentioned information also applies if your investigation involves the alleged patient abuse and neglect of a developmentally disabled vulnerable adult. Some examples of records also needed in these cases are any and all information on the level of mental retardation of the reported victim and results of recent inspections by the appropriate State agencies. Look for any and all reports filed against the company owning the particular "group home" in which the patient abuse or neglect has allegedly occurred. A significant amount of developmentally disabled adults have been placed within the community in various "group homes." In most cases these group homes are located literally smack in the middle of the residential community. Thus, you may have potential witnesses to criminal neglect in the form of not only other caregivers but citizen "neighbors," which our office had by the way. You should obtain the group home staffing records covering the window of opportunity for the alleged criminal activity. These group homes often have a caregiver actually living full-time with the patients. In these cases the patients are often referred to not as "patients" but as "clients." Regardless, these people are vulnerable adults. The group home must also keep detailed records on the rotation of caregivers assigned to the clients.

The staff must keep records on any and all "Unusual Activities," which are also often referred to as "episodes," occurring during the respective caregiver's tour of duty.

You may recall the "real cases and real faces" example we addressed earlier in the book pertaining to the developmentally disabled vulnerable adult who was found to have sustained serious bruising to his legs and buttocks. In this particular case the caregiver to the victim failed to document any unusual activity or episode occurring during the time he was assigned to care for the victim. Why? He failed to report his criminal attack on the victim with a shoe and a belt and, thus, inflicting serious visible injuries to the victim's legs and buttocks.

Beware, patient abuse and neglect can and will also happen in "day care" centers. Often these day care centers are, as most "providers" of care, "Medicaid" funded and thus, fall under the jurisdiction of the respective Medicaid Fraud Control Unit. Records must also be kept on outside the group home activities, such as attendance at centers that provide daily activities of living to the "clients" during the day. These are often referred to as "Community Outings." Except in the most severe cases of mental disability, the "clients" are normally out of the group home during the day. So you will have to conduct a multiple site investigation. Of course, this results in the necessity to gather records from multiple locations in preparation for your interview. As we discussed earlier the investigator must have a copy of the client's medical documentation relative to his/her level of mental disability. You see, most of the clients while physically full grown "adults" often have the mental age of small children or even infants. Thus, they pose a real physical challenge to caregivers. These victims are subjected to all types of abuse including physical, sexual, emotional and financial abuse, as well as neglect. In one case, our Medicaid Fraud Control Unit investigators had a client who was on the "record" as purchasing a personal computer and very expensive athletic shoes. This would be fine, if the client could actually use the items, however, due to the client's mental and physical disabilities, as documented in records obtained and reviewed by the investigators prior to suspect interviews, the items were useless. However, they were far from "useless" to the caregiver who, of course, really enjoyed the personal computer and the very expensive "in vogue" athletic shoes. In summary, follow the document trail, obtain the records prior to the suspect interview and pull them out at a strategic point in the interview and confront the suspect.

Also, as I have said over and over again, you **must** obtain any and all photographs taken of the victim's injuries. Of course, this applies to all victims be they developmentally disabled or elderly vulnerable adults residing in nursing homes or other care settings.

In summary, you may want to refer back to Chapter Five for additional details. You must be prepared prior to the interview of your suspect. Ideally, you should give the suspect the impression that you know much, much more about him/her and the incident that you are investigating than you actually know.

THE SUSPECT INTERVIEW

In cases where the suspect has not, as yet, retained an attorney, he/she is fair game as far as I am concerned. I **never** schedule the interview of the suspect. I want the element of surprise on my side. What do you think would occur if I sent the suspect a letter or finally reached him/her by phone? Of course, you know the answer, NOTHING! They would trash the letter and slam the phone down in my ear! In an overwhelming amount of cases, we are not talking about professionals here such as doctors or Registered Nurses, etc., who have highly sought after and difficult to obtain professional certifications and education to protect. In all my years conducting cases in this manner, I can count on one hand the suspects who declined to speak with me. There were times, after coordination with the DN, I interviewed the suspect while he/she was actually working at the care setting. In addition, and remarkably, most times I was standing on the suspect's door step with my badge and identification in hand and they still freely admitted me into their homes. True case example: I went to a suspect's home early in the morning before dawn watching for signs of early morning activity. It was a work day at about 7:15 a.m., when I knocked on the apartment door. The suspect answered the door. As we discussed, while he knew he had been accused of patient abuse during the Internal Investigation and was suspended, he had no clue that I was looking for him. I clearly displayed my Office of the Attorney General badge and also gave him my business card. Both actions should have been clear notice to him of just who I was, for whom I worked, and that he was a suspect in the criminal abuse of a vulnerable adult. He still allowed me to enter his home. I then proceeded to conduct his suspect interview. I did not provide the suspect with his Miranda Warning, although as we discussed, I reminded him that I was a guest in his home and he could request that I end the interview at any time and I would end it without question. Finally, after some time, and after I had already obtained numerous inconsistent statements, the suspect asked me, "Who are you?" I again displayed my official Office of the Attorney General (OAG) identification and reminded him that I had also done so prior to entering his home. At this point the suspect advised me that he did not think he should talk to me. Of course, I stopped the interview and noted the date and time. This suspect was later successfully prosecuted by our legal staff in the form of Assistant Attorney General Timothy U. Sharpe.

Another "real cases and real faces" example for your review involved a female suspect who had been accused of physically attacking several developmentally disabled vulnerable adults under her care. The vulnerable adults sustained visible injuries including a broken thumb. You may recall that we spoke about "group homes" being placed in the midst of residential communities and, thus, you may run across "neighbors" as witnesses. Well, in this case, not only did we have neighbor witnesses, but also one who actually physically intervened on behalf of one of the victims. The suspect was witnessed pushing one vulnerable adult to the ground. This all took place in the yard of the group home. The suspect was raising a lawn chair over the head of one of the vulnerable adults when a "neighbor witness" intervened preventing further assault and most likely additional injuries to the victims under the care of the suspect. After numerous attempts to gain a response at the suspect's apartment door, I decided to "wait her out." I had already verified her residence via the apartment office manager. So, it came to pass that one very early morning (prior to 6:00 a.m.), I literally sat on the steps outside her apartment door as her neighbors came and went and we exchanged "Good Mornings." Finally, the suspect, who I could also visually identify, came out of her apartment door to my "Good Morning" face as I displayed my official identification. Again, as in the overwhelming number of cases, the suspect still invited me into her home. An hour into the interview I had what I needed and ended the interview. I suggest that at the end of an interview that you actually opt to end, you document that fact. We later charged the suspect and she was found guilty on numerous counts of Patient Abuse and Assault & Battery. At one point in the proceedings the suspect now a defendant, uttered a threat directed towards our prosecutor, Assistant Attorney General Catherine Schuster Pascale. The judge ordered a Pre-Sentence Investigation (PSI) be conducted. At the PSI Hearing the judge came down hard on the defendant citing such things as her display of complete lack of remorse. The judge then ordered the defendant to be placed under arrest and taken to jail directly from the Courtroom. At times, to "reach and speak" with the suspect you must be innovative and a bit tenacious. Once again, while this works for me you must do what works for you and at the direction of you supervisory legal staff.

Another "real cases and real faces" example elucidates the proven and time honored benefit of "case notes" and operating in an environment the investigator does not control. Case Notes or "notes." you must take them and they must be accurate! While you should have a list of issues and specific questions you want answered by the suspect you must, during the interview, also document events occurring during the interview. Such as the beginning and ending times, any breaks taken, and who else may be in the room the entire time or just "passing through." Remember, you are in their home. True case example of "environment," I had a case that occurred in rural western Maryland. If not for the assistance of the local law enforcement Detective Sergeant assigned to assist me, I would still be looking for the rural home of our only eyewitness! Right in the middle of the interview, the witness's adult daughter walked between me and the witness and stood there for a moment. The witness's daughter heard us speaking about the suspect. The daughter, who was still standing between me and her mother, our key witness, said words to the effect, "Everybody knows 'so and so,' the suspect. We have a social club here and we don't allow her in because we don't like all her (suspect's) 'profound statements.'" Of course, the young lady meant to refer to the suspect's use of "profanity" but it was a difficult moment for me and the Detective Sergeant, who knew all the parties in the case from the victim to the suspect and all in between. It was a small town. I documented the interruption of the daughter and time during the interview she entered and left the room. **Also remember your case notes can end up in the hands of the defense at trial.** Accuracy is paramount! This case was later successfully prosecuted by former Assistant Attorney General Timothy U. Sharpe.

Another true case example of accurate "notes" involved another case I had, this time in deep southern Maryland. Previous "networking" also paid off in this case. I knew the suspect was still employed by the facility while the Internal Investigation continued. In this case the location of the alleged incidents was a Veteran's Home. Although we had several "weak" witnesses, the victims were all physically and mentally disabled and could not undergo the rigors of an interview, let alone testimony at trial. The networking paid off in several ways. I verified that the suspect, who was an "orderly" and not a Certified Nursing Assistant, was working as I spoke by phone with the Director of Nursing. I had dealt with the Director of Nursing years before. I explained to the DN that I needed her cooperation by **not informing** the suspect that I was coming to the facility to interview him. I did not feel like a nearly four hour, ride, one way, only to find the suspect had called off sick after being told by the DN that I was coming. If the suspect did not want to speak with me fine. I just wanted to look him in the eye when he respectfully declined. The DN complied and also agreed to allow me to conduct the interview in her office. The suspect was simply called to report to the office of the DN with no further explanation. When the suspect, who was approximately 6'4 and well over 250 lbs., entered the room, he was introduced to me by the DN and she left us alone in her office.

After the standard introduction, providing the suspect with my identification and badge, he consented to my interview. Although I did not provide him his Miranda Warning, he knew who I was, where I worked and what I wanted to discuss. He also knew, as in all my interviews of suspects, that he could end the interview at any time without question. After about 45 minutes, and with only some minor damage inflicted to his story, I decided to end the interview. As I stood expressing that the interview was now over, the suspect seemed confused as to the ending. He asked me what would happen now. I informed him that I was hungry and that I was going to look for a good restaurant. He then asked me what would happen then. I told him that after eating I would return to my Baltimore office and prepare a Statement of Charges and Charging Documents formally placing criminal charges against him for the physical Abuse (Assault & Battery) of specified patients of the Veteran's Nursing Home.

At this point in the now "closed" interview I was standing between the suspect and the door with my hand on the door knob beginning to open the door. The suspect then uttered a "spontaneous admission of guilt" by stating words to the effect that he did do what he had been accused of doing, that is, pulling hard on the ears of wheelchair bound patients, "flicking" their ears with his fingers, slapping them and throwing food in their faces, etc. All these acts meet the elements of Maryland law for criminal charges. I then resumed the interview and obtained some additional details before again ending the interview. Our office did place criminal charges against the suspect.

Later, trial was held in a southern Maryland District Court. As usual the witnesses were sequestered and I was the last witness for the State. After the defendant testified and left the stand, I was then called into court to testify. The first thing I did before being sworn in was to look into the eyes of my prosecutor, Assistant Attorney General Timothy U. Sharpe. This convinced me that all would be well, and just to go with it. The defense attorney then approached me. Before I proceed, it must be said that this attorney did a fine job in defending his client. The defense attorney said words to the effect, "Sir, you come to this Court with impeccable credentials." At this, all of my defense shields went into action because I knew what was to follow, and that was a direct attack on my so stated "impeccable credentials" by the defense attorney, who had just referred to them in open court. The defense attorney then demanded loudly that was it not true that I used "coercion" and even "tricked" his client into his confession during my over one hour and a half interview? He added that I also physically "blocked" the defendant's exit from the small office and, in fact, prohibited his freely leaving until I obtained his confession. First of all, and it was all backed up with my notes, my interview which I ended, lasted about 45 minutes. Yes, I was standing between the door and the defendant, but it was he who opted to continue the interview after I advised him it was over. My prosecutor then asked me a series of questions establishing the fact that I was old enough to be the defendant's father and that he out weighed me by almost one hundred pounds. Finally, the judge said, enough. It was clear to the court that the prosecutor had made his points. The judge then asked me directly if it was true that I had a record of obtaining "a lot" of confessions or admissions of guilt. I respectfully advised the judge that it all depended on what is meant by a "lot" since I had been in the field, at that time, for over twenty-five years, but I did not think of the number one way or the other. I just went from case to case, face to face and year to year, seeking the truth and preparing the best case possible for my supervisory attorneys. What was the end result of the case? Guilty on all counts.

In conclusion, the interview of the suspect in a criminal investigation is always decisive. The suspect interview can result in the establishment that there is indeed probable cause to believe that a crime has been committed and by that particular suspect, and further, that criminal charges should be placed. However, the suspect interview can take many twists and turns, and the investigator must be prepared to face them. For the information of those readers not in the profession of law enforcement, contrary to depictions via the entertainment world, suspects just don't "roll over" and confess.

Criminal investigators must always remember that they seek the truth and not be influenced by the need to increase statistics or "clearance rates." Criminal investigators must be diligent in the pursuit of their cases. Remember time is never on the criminal investigators side. "Patient abuse and neglect cases don't age like fine wine." You must be prepared to pursue these cases in a much different manner than a criminal fraud case or other "white collar crime" cases.

You must take accurate "notes" during the interview and be prepared to find them in the hands of the defense during pre-trial negotiations and at trial. You must be both persistent and consistent. You must control the interview and not let the suspect control it, even when the interview takes place on the suspect's turf. Miranda Warnings should be provided to the suspect only if required by law. Simply put, the criminal investigator must know when it is necessary provide the Miranda Warning and when it is not.

Use of the Polygraph Examination

This section of the book will briefly address some of the key issues involving the use of polygraph examinations by law enforcement and prosecutors. Those professionals out there in the law enforcement world will need to follow their own respective Policies and Procedures regarding the use of polygraph examinations. I will not insult your knowledge and expertise in the use of polygraph examinations by assuming that you need additional information from this writer. This section of the book will benefit those non-law enforcement professionals so that they can gain a better understanding of the often "mythical" polygraph examination. We have all heard about "polygraphs" and, thus, have developed our own respective opinions on the positive and or negative effects of the use of polygraph examinations. Of course, those of us in the law enforcement field can cite numerous examples of when the "box" worked and when the "box" failed. It is not an exact science, to say the least. Is the polygraph a good "tool" to use during criminal investigations? Yes, very much so. The keys to the successful use of the polygraph examination include some of the "keys" we have previously addressed in this book.

It should be noted, there have been numerous books published about polygraph examinations, and the following is only a brief overview for the information for the reader. I have always considered the use of polygraph examinations as one of the basic "tools" used in constructing the case "building block" analogy we have addressed in this book.

1. **Preparation, preparation and more preparation**. You must establish the actual need or benefit of offering a suspect the opportunity of taking a polygraph examination. "Opportunity" a word I often use to my suspects. Like I'm "giving" them something when, in fact, I am giving them nothing.

2. **Don't offer the polygraph examination unless you feel actual need for it.**

3. In some states the results of a polygraph examination **can not** be presented during a criminal proceeding.

4. There are several basic types of suspect "profiles" as pertaining to agreeing to submit to a polygraph examination. Some think they can "beat" the box. I like this type the most because their arrogance often leads to their downfall. Then there are the types that say they will take the polygraph examination without me even offering them the "opportunity." However, in most cases, somehow things change between the scheduling date and the actual examination. Specifically, this type of suspect fails to show. Lastly, there is the suspect who says he wants to take

the polygraph examination, shows up for the examination, goes through the "pre test" phase, takes the examination and no deception is detected. Of course, as you know, the polygraph does not detect "lies" but can find and measure degrees and points of "deception."

5. The "pre-test" phase of the polygraph examination can often be the most critical. Why? In a significant number of cases, it is during this phase, before the formal polygraph examination is even started that the suspect "gives it up" and asks to speak to the investigator before the examiner proceeds. It is at this point that the suspect often utters admissions of guilt. Another option for the suspect is just to end the "opportunity" and leave.

State Medicaid Fraud Control Units (SMFCUs)

It is also my opinion, which can be backed up by statistics kept by the National Association of Medicaid Fraud Control Units, that the respective Medicaid Fraud Control Unit (MFCU) is an excellent office for regulatory agencies even the providers to refer these cases. After years of successful networking with others in the official "loop" of notification of patient abuse and neglect in Maryland, it became the norm for our office, which was not in the reporting "loop" officially, to receive almost daily referrals **directly** from the providers of care, the police, Long Term Care Ombudsman (LTCO) and State Health Department. We became a member of the notification "club" by "reputation" and productivity, rather than by regulatory laws. Again, not to sound critical of the response of the local police, but they are often not equipped to handle these cases beyond the initial report. Their sergeants are often screaming for them to get "back on the road." Over the years we did make some significant progress with some law enforcement agencies. We provided on-the-job training to detectives who were, for a period of time, assigned to us for joint training and working actual cases with our unit. Some agencies have even established small patient abuse and neglect units within their Child Abuse Units. Why? The victims are so similar. The victims often can not be reliable witnesses for themselves and there are often no "reported" eye witnesses or there are "reluctant" eye witnesses. In Maryland, our original patient abuse and neglect criminal cite was more or less patterned after our "Child Abuse" law. Why? Again, the victims of these crimes are so similar. Over the years it has been amended to, in my opinion, better protect our vulnerable adults.

Some reasons to refer complaints of alleged Patient Abuse and Neglect to the MFCU (Medicaid Fraud Control Unit)

The enactment of the Medicare and Medicaid Anti-Fraud and Abuse Amendments authorized the establishment of and Federal funding for the State Medicaid Fraud Control Units (SMFCUs). Currently, forty-seven states and the District of Columbia participate in the Medicaid fraud control giant program through their establishment of SMFCUs. The majority of the units are located within the respective States' Office of the Attorney General. A small number of the units are located within other State Agencies. The mission of the Medicaid Fraud Control Unit is to investigate and prosecute Medicaid provider fraud, as well as incidents of patient abuse and neglect. The U.S. Department of Health and Human Services, (HHS), Office of the Inspector General (OIG), delegates the authority annually to certify each SMFCU as eligible to receive Federal grant funds under the Medicaid Fraud control program. The Medicaid Fraud Control Units receive 90 percent Federal funding for the first three years of operation and 75 percent thereafter. A primary goal of the OIG is to ensure that each unit fully complies with all Federal regulations governing the functions and operations of the Medicaid Fraud Control Unit.

The Medicaid Fraud Control Unit (MFCU) has experienced staff dedicated to the investigation and prosecution of patient abuse and neglect and has Federal Laws authorizing the unit's specific role in investigating both Medicaid Fraud and the Abuse and Neglect of vulnerable adults occurring in facilities that are Medicaid funded. Most nursing homes and other care providers are indeed Medicaid funded.

Experience: Most MFCUs have well over fifteen years experience investigating and, when appropriate, prosecuting these cases. The MFCUs know the Long Term Care Facility (LTCF) and Mentally Disabled care facilities "world." They know what records to obtain and take into evidence. They know the setting or arena, so to speak. Of course, they have time to conduct in-depth investigations including interviews and interrogations as appropriate. And, finally, they have experienced legal staff to present findings and prosecute criminal cases or, when appropriate, refer them back to regulatory agencies for adjudication at the Administrative Hearing level.

Local States' Attorney's Offices (SAO) suffer a constant case overload at all levels, especially the "lower" court or the "District Court" and also in the "higher" court level the "Circuit Court" (Maryland). At the District Court level of Maryland, it is not uncommon for the Assistant State's Attorney (ASA) to have his/her first review of the case the day of the trial when the ASA literally "opens" the case file. The ASA, at times, starts the day with 40-50 cases on the morning Court Docket alone. However, both levels have heavy case loads. The local prosecutors have their hands full with not only more cases on their daily docket, but cases at the felony level, such as murders, rapes, armed robberies, etc. In most cases, the local SAO gladly defers patient abuse and neglect cases to the respective Medicaid Fraud Control Unit.

The MFCUs have had years to establish a professional rapport with other agencies in the reporting loop. Specifically, the MFCU deals almost daily with the State Health Department, the State Long Term Care Ombudsman, local and state law enforcement agencies, and even the "Providers" of care, such as nursing homes caring for elderly infirmed vulnerable adults and "group homes" for the mentally disabled vulnerable adults. The MFCUs have crossed-trained at both the local and national level.

Suggestions to Administrative staff on how to conduct an Internal Investigation

Before we proceed to the next section, and for the record, I don't have the skills of Provider Administrative staff or Nursing supervisory staff and I don't expect them to have the skills necessary to conduct a criminal investigation nor should they attempt to conduct a criminal investigation. However, as I have repeatedly stated over these many years, when we work together, we can make the system produce much more accurate Incident Reports or Internal Investigations, which are so important in the building blocks. Over the years and following thousands of referrals and hundreds of investigations our networking and training of provider management and supervisory staff paid off, to say the least. One may ask why? Although not part of the actual open criminal investigation beyond the "Incident or Accident Report," the `investigations conducted at the level of the provider can provide excellent "building blocks" on which a criminal investigation can later be built. However, as we proceed, I will provide you with examples of when things went wrong during the "Incident or Accident Report" level investigation. We can all learn by our mistakes.

The very first thing provider management must do is follow the directions of the "Suggested Checklist" in Chapter Three. If not, develop another "form" that provides the same information to follow-up investigators such as the Office of the Attorney General-Medicaid Fraud Control Unit-Patient Abuse Coordinator. This will establish uniformity in the documentation and reporting to outside agencies of allegations of patient abuse and neglect. Management must train and assign specific staff to conduct and/or supervise the investigations of patient abuse and neglect occurring within the facility. As you may recall, Maryland's Office of the Attorney General-Medicaid Fraud Control Unit, as part of our outreach and networking programs, has been training provider staff since 1989.

The "Suggested Checklist" can be a guide post or outline for enabling the facility to document much of the "who, what, where, when and why" of the individual incident report or allegation of patient abuse and neglect. Again, please see Chapter Three for more details on the "Suggested Checklist."

The provider facility must establish clear and concise Policies and Procedures on Patient Abuse and Neglect Prevention and Investigative Procedures. The Policy and Procedures must clearly list the outside agencies that must be notified of the alleged patient abuse and neglect. Caregivers and other staff having access to vulnerable adults must be required to actually "sign off" acknowledging the facility's Policies and Procedures regarding patient abuse and neglect. These records can later be very useful to the facility in taking administrative actions against staff. These records can, as you may recall, also be very important at trial or during regulatory administrative hearings as the prosecutor presents them during the proceedings.

Although some of the below information is also explained in Chapter One, it is expanded on and described in much more detail here to assist Administrators, Managers and Supervisors of nursing homes or other facilities in conducting Internal Investigations of allegations of patient abuse and neglect. It must also be noted that the definitions provided in this book originate from various sources such as my lessons plans and Maryland's criminal and regulatory cites. Each respective state has its own definitions and cites, so it is important to become familiar with the laws and regulations of your own state. However, the "basics" are often very similar. One common thread remains that the states are bound by the myriad of Federal regulatory cites. We also share the common responsibility of protecting our "vulnerable."

Physical Abuse: The provider policy must define and list the types of patient abuse and neglect, such as physical attacks, sexual attacks, emotional abuse and financial abuse. We have previously provided some examples, but I will expand them here. Physical abuse is most often an intentional, provoked or unprovoked, attack on a vulnerable adult. Some examples are slapping, punching, choking, pinching, spitting upon, force feeding, and throwing the patient to the floor. I have seen them all and more. In fact, I have had suspect caregivers freely and without any remorse say to me that yes they did indeed slap or punch their patient because the patient had hit them or spat upon them. The fact that their patient was very elderly, frail and suffered from one of the many forms of dementia was completely lost on the suspect "caregivers." This is why caregivers must be continuously trained on how to care for vulnerable adults who often suffer from Alzheimer's or other such conditions that alter their mental health and often their responses to care. As we have discussed, the caregivers must be aware of the Care Plan of the patient. Why? The Care Plan should contain information that directly addresses "hands on" care issues. The caregivers must learn that, even if the vulnerable adult male Alzheimer's patient is a 6'4 and over 200 pounds and the caregiver is 5'3 and 110 pounds, the patient is still the "vulnerable adult." It is not pleasant, not pleasant at all to be spat upon or struck by a vulnerable adult. I say this because I know from personal experience. However, caregiver staff must learn that spitting on or physically assaulting the vulnerable adult is not only wrong, it is also a criminal act.

Sexual Abuse: Sexual Abuse is almost self-explanatory and I have provided an example previously in this book. Can Sexual Abuse occur in any facility and at any time? You bet it can. I even had a case involving a female caregiver sexually abusing female patients. Example of "Real cases and real faces:" In this case a female caregiver was accused of sexually abusing three very elderly, frail, and vulnerable adult females. My investigation revealed that during "personal" care such as diaper changing or bathing the female caregiver sexually abused three vulnerable adult female patients under her care. Two of the victims, although suffering from various physical infirmities, were very alert and coherent. After several interviews and meetings with them and their families it was clear that two of the victims were very consistent and could qualify as reliable witnesses for themselves. The third female victim, who had suffered a stroke and was very limited in her mobility, could not speak. I had to call a local law enforcement agency and borrow from their Child Abuse Unit some "anatomically correct" dolls to utilize during my interview of the third victim. However, prior to trial we met with the physician of the victims. The doctor understood our position but he added "at what price justice?" While the victims were coherent and could testify, the doctor was frank saying he did not want to have his patients die on the stand. The doctor had a very good point and we respected it. However, we still took the case to trial utilizing other forms of evidence and, in fact. our legal staff did prevail. Later the defendant appealed to the next higher Court in Maryland, the "Circuit Court", and our case was up-held and in fact the Circuit Judge increased the penalties set down in the lower Court!

The bottom line is that this insidious crime can and will occur in facilities caring for our vulnerable adults. What do the suspects look like? Take a look in your mirror. They look like you and me! They are young and, as I have explained in a previous "real cases and faces" case, old. Suspects can be professionals and caregivers at all levels. They can be employees, agency staff, and even volunteers! Provider management staff, while not criminal investigators, must learn to treat the rooms in which these crimes take place as "crime scenes" until the first responders, the police, arrive. Please, I'm not saying place "crime scene tape" all around, but I do suggest you keep people out of the room. Also don't have staff remove the victim's clothing and bedding etc., and take them to the laundry room! (This has happened.) The police will know what steps to take such as having a reported sexual assault victim treated and examined by a physician (Rape Kit). The police will know what items in the crime scene to take into evidence in order to establish a "Chain of Custody," which is so fundamental later at a criminal proceeding. No "fruit of the poisonous tree" evidence please!

You may recall early on in this book I respectfully advised that this effort would not be a book about statistics and charts. I also advised that it was not a "law book." However, in the interest of stressing the absolute importance of proper "chain of custody" and how the provider/nursing home levels can play roles in it, I will briefly explain the "poisonous tree" circumstances and how "poisonous tree" evidence can kill a criminal case. There are nearly endless examples I could furnish based on all my years in this profession but the easiest one is the "Miranda Warning." Should a law enforcement officer fail to provide a suspect his/her Miranda Warning when called for and proceeds with the interview, any and all incriminating statements, confessions or admissions of guilt and even physical evidence are in serious jeopardy at trial, if it even gets that far. Why? The statements and other evidence become the "fruit of the poisonous tree" when the police conducted the suspect interview without providing the suspect with his/her "Miranda Warning" rights. Other more complicated examples deal with probable cause to believe a crime has been committed issues and violations of our Constitutional rights as they pertain to "unreasonable searches and seizures." One example is when a law enforcement officer makes an improper arrest, not based on sufficient "probable cause" to believe that the person whom he/she arrested did, in fact, commit the crime. Another example, is when law enforcement officers conduct improper and unauthorized "searches and seizures" of a suspect's "person" or "property" in violation of the Fourth Amendment to the Constitution of the United States of America.

Emotional Abuse: While this type of patient abuse is often not a "crime" in most states, it is nonetheless one of the more prevalent, mean-spirited, vicious and painful types of all the forms of "abuse." It can come in many forms. You may recall early on in this book when I referred to one of my repeated refrains over these many years that "Patient abuse and neglect are many things to many people but always the same to the victim." Emotional Abuse also falls into this description. While often not a "criminal act" and difficult to define, these acts are always humiliating and emotionally painful to the coherent vulnerable adult victims. Some examples would include: screaming at and calling the victims derogatory names, intentionally failing to answer the call button and then yelling at the patient not to use it again, and ridiculing the victim. Years ago I recall a case, which was prosecuted in criminal court in another state. This particular case involved a vulnerable adult female, who had limited mobility, being taunted and teased by several caregivers. The abuse reached its lowest point when the female caregivers turned their backs on the victim and in unison "mooned" the victim. Another graphic case, also prosecuted in another state, involved a very sad and tragic case of emotional abuse of an elderly and confused female patient. We have all have seen elderly female patients carry "baby dolls" around the facility. At times the patient's room has a crib for the "baby" to sleep in. For all intents and purposes, these "baby dolls" are "living human beings" to the patient. Well, in this particularly tragic and painful case, an employee, who was not a direct caregiver, thought it would be rather humorous to take the "baby doll" and hang it from the ceiling. Of course, when discovered by the victim she suffered the death and loss of her "baby." You can imagine the horror the patient experienced as she screamed finding her "baby" dead and "hanging" from the ceiling. Sad, very, sad. Some other examples border on "Criminal Neglect," such as intentionally withholding food and water after the victim has had some type of "accident" such as bedwetting. The "withholding" in this form of emotional abuse is meant as "punishment."

Financial Abuse: This type of abuse comes in the form of any and all types of fraud, misappropriation or theft of the patient's personal funds. Some examples include stealing the patient's Social Security checks, Veteran's Disability checks, or other forms of incoming monetary funds. It also includes documenting that the facility purchased personal necessities for the patient such as clothing and toiletries, etc., when the funds were actually criminally diverted for the personal use of the suspect. The financial abuse can come in any illegal form which results in the patient being deprived of the funds or the items the funds were designated to purchase for the victim's personal care and human needs and wants. You may recall an earlier example I provided wherein very expensive personal items, which were documented as being purchased for a developmentally disabled vulnerable adult, but because of his infirmities, he could never possibly use, were later revealed to have been diverted to the personal property and use of the suspect caregiver. Financial abuse can be occasional or isolated in nature or an organized and systemic effort that extends throughout the facility or organization. In this type of abuse, we are talking about extensive and complicated investigations entailing the obtaining of many financial documents and the expertise of auditors and other specialists. **In criminal physical and sexual abuse cases the investigations often come down to the testimony of "people" then augmented by documentation. In the cases of financial abuse or fraud the investigations often come down to the gathering of relevant financial documents and then augmented by the testimony of "people."**

The provider must also present to staff in the Policy and Procedures, the definitions and examples of Patient "Neglect." Neglect means the intentional failure to provide the necessary assistance and resources for the physical needs of a vulnerable adult. Some examples which should be explained in the Policy are:

A. Failure to provide proper positioning and turning

B. Failure to provide proper hygiene

C. Failure to provide proper hydration

D. Failure to provide nutrition

E. Failure to provide proper clothing

F. Failure to provide proper toileting: This can be both physically and emotionally damaging to the patient. Just stop and think about it for a moment. What can be more humiliating than having an "accident" (BM) because your caregiver repeatedly failed to respond to your call button for assistance? This failure to provide proper care, as all the professional nurses out there know, can be catastrophic to patients with pressure sores.

G. Failure to provide proper supervision: You may recall we have already addressed this type of neglect as part of my "real cases and real faces." However, I will for the benefit of the reader provide another example of "real cases and real faces" relative to the Criminal Neglect of vulnerable adults. In this particular case the five victims, who were all developmentally disabled vulnerable adults, were both physically and mentally infirmed. Some were both mentally retarded and physically handicapped, necessitating the use of crutches and/or walkers. This case was not only sad and tragic for the victims and their families but also somewhat "spectacular." Let me explain. You see, the "alleged" criminal neglect in the form of lack of proper supervision was captured on tape by a Washington, DC Television Station. A former employee, who felt he was wrongfully terminated by the Provider, went to the press rather than the police to report alleged acts of neglect committed by staff employed by the Provider. He also alleged the improper use of the Provider's vehicles for personal errands by staff, as the patients ("clients" in this case) remained out in the vans and for some period of time unsupervised. This form of patient abuse and neglect, failure to provide supervision, along with injuring the "clients" while providing bathing, are prevalent examples of this crime occurring in group homes. In the case of bathing tragically, because the caregivers turn the water heater temperature up much too high, over 130 degrees, the clients sustain serious and, at times, fatal burns.

Back to this sad example of Patient Neglect: This incident of lack of proper supervision occurred in a very hot month of June. The caregivers had the clients out of the facility for a "Community Outing," taking clients out into shopping centers, malls, and parks, etc. Since this particular day was so very hot, the caregivers took the clients to another group home "safe house" to keep them out of the heat. Remember, at the time they were unknowingly being followed by the press with video cameras running. The two female caregivers did, in fact, take the clients to the group home as instructed and took them inside out of the heat. However, after a time the five vulnerable adult victims were videotaped exiting the group home alone and completely unsupervised. The two female caregivers were nowhere to be seen on the tape. Please, recall that we are talking about both physically and mentally disabled adults in this case. One of the victims was recorded, and let me tell you it was difficult to observe, crawling on her hands and knees down the handicap ramp of the group home and across the gravel driveway and finally painfully climbing up into the van. This is not the end of the story. You may recall, my explaining that it was a very hot day; according to the National Weather Service, it was nearly record-breaking. Once the clients were all in the parked van, which was not running, they remained in the van completely unsupervised for over 30 minutes! What were the caregivers doing inside the air conditioned group home as their clients were outside in the heat inside a very hot van? Who knows? Does it really matter? What matters is that the two trained and experienced caregivers completely failed to provide the victims with the very basic of care, supervision. We conducted several unscientific tests on a hot day with a similar van and the temperature inside was well over 100 degrees. The videotaped evidence was presented to our office directly by the Washington, DC Television Station. This incident occurred in Prince George's County, Maryland, a Washington, DC suburb. Along with the videotape evidence we also had the former employee eye witness and, of course, the testimony of the press professionals covering the story.

Did our office proceed with a criminal investigation? Yes. Did our office place formal charges against the two female caregivers? You bet we did. Did we "win" the case at trial? Yes and no. This case, or should I say these cases since we had two defendants, became one of our only three losses over all my years as the Patient Abuse Unit-Patient Abuse Coordinator (PAC). It was what I later called our "50/50 case," meaning we lost one case and won the other. Specifically, one of the defendants pleaded guilty, while the other opted to stand trial. How could one of the best Offices of the Attorney General in the entire United States not be totally victorious with the actual "crime" presented to the court via videotape? In this case, even after being explained the elements of the crime very clearly and profoundly by our prosecutor, along with all the overwhelming evidence, the court still completely lost track as to what "patient neglect" was and was not. In short, the court acquitted the second defendant on all counts.

The reason? Although we clearly provided the court with a rock solid case of "Criminal Neglect." the court advised we charged the wrong persons! The court was of the opinion that the crime shown was committed not by the assigned, experienced caregivers, who were "there" and had been assigned to care for the clients, but by the persons in "management" of the group home. The court thought we should have placed criminal charges against the "corporation." Do you now see why I said that the court had "lost track" of the understanding of the "elements" of the crime? We have discussed "systemic" Criminal Neglect wherein the "facility" management committed the crimes by means of cutting services, cutting staff, cutting nurse supervisory staff, thus leading to the widespread medical problems and the criminal neglect of their patients. The case I have described in this "real cases and real faces" was a crystal clear case against the two assigned and experienced caregivers and not the corporation. Regardless, we pursued "righteous" cases and in the end our office "won" as did the citizens of Maryland by bringing the cases to trial.

H. Failure to report any "accidents" occurring during patient care. We have addressed this previously in an example of how a caregiver can and will be prosecuted for the crime of Criminal Neglect, when he/she fails to report accidentally dropping the patient to the floor but instead just picks up the patient and places the incoherent and most likely injured patient back into bed. As I have often cautioned caregivers during training, please, **don't become a criminal, when you only had an accident"** with your patient. Facing any administrative actions is far better than standing in a Courtroom as the Judge comes in to hear the State vs. you!

I. Failure to provide proper shelter

J. Failure to provide medical treatment: An example of this type of "neglect" is when caregivers intentionally divert controlled dangerous substance medications for their own personal use and, thus, deny them to the patient. Can you imagine the pain patients endure without the proper dosage of morphine for their near end-of-life pain? Another type could be part of systemic problems within the facility resulting from intentional acts coming from the very "top" of management, such as cut-backs in necessary nursing staff, caregivers and durable medical equipment. These intentional cut-backs can and will result in the intentional "neglect" of the patients under their care.

Recent headlines also reflect "neglect" in the form of the much more serious "negligent" homicide. I refer to the tragic case that occurred in New Orleans during the terrible storm "Katrina." You may recall that 34 patients in a "nursing home" perished as the flood waters raged on. In a story dated September 9, 2006, The "Baltimore Sun," the owners of the nursing home, who face a myriad of charges, are suing the government both State and Federal levels, "saying that federal, State, and local officials failed to make sure vulnerable citizens were evacuated as the storm approached." On September 20, 2006, the owners were indicted and faced multiple criminal charges. Again, my endless refrain over all these many years, "Patient abuse and neglect are many things to many people, but always the same to the victim."

In this book, we have discussed criminal cases we prosecuted involving outrageous acts of "neglect" by assigned caregivers. Some of these outrageous cases occurred in group homes for developmentally disabled adults. Some examples: vulnerable adults left alone and completely unsupervised in a parked van on one of the hottest days of a very long and hot summer, completely vulnerable adults who were blind and deaf with the mental ages of small children at most, being abandoned in the suspect caregiver's apartment which caught fire during the abandonment, once again vulnerable adults being intentionally abandoned by their caregiver as she went out to conduct personal business. And the group home caught fire as a direct result of the scented candles she lit to cover up the overwhelming smell of urine! I could provide more examples. Over these many years I have repeatedly cautioned regulatory and prosecutorial professionals that, although we have successfully investigated and prosecuted allegations of patient abuse and neglect occurring in group homes for developmentally disabled vulnerable adults, we have barely scratched the surface. In "nursing homes" we have professional nursing staff on duty 24 hours a day. Nursing homes also provide structured care environments. In "group homes" the staff has far less formal training, are underpaid, and, at times, lack an effective span of supervisory control over the vulnerable adults assigned to their care. It was also my experience that the "supervisors" of these "group homes" at times went "unsupervised." That is not to say that there are not good and nurturing group home care settings out there, because there are. However, it has been my personal experience over the years that these settings, at times, do not provide the good and nurturing care management intends.

Some things "to do" and "not to do" while conducting Internal Investigations

Here I will recommend to provider management some things "to do" and "not to do" while conducting investigations into "Incident and Accident Reports" of patient abuse and neglect. These recommendations and examples expand over my entire career in this field. I will provide examples of how Internal Investigations can, at times, make or break successful criminal prosecutions. Of course, I also realize the provider/facility must follow the advice of their legal staff. This list is also not meant to be all inclusive.

1. Do: As we have already stated, the provider/facility must have clear and concise Policy and Procedures and have them available for all staff.

2. Do: Have a standard and uniform report form such as the "Suggested Checklist."

3. Do: Have a specific and trained person(s) at the supervisory level from Nursing and Human Resources/Risk Management responsible for conducting the Internal Investigation. These staff members can act as liaisons between the provider/facility and outside agencies.

4. Do: Establish and, most importantly, maintain professional rapport with others in the reporting "loop," such as the State Health Department, The Long Term Care Ombudsman, Law Enforcement, and I hope the Office of the Attorney General—Medicaid Fraud Control Unit—Patient Abuse Unit.

5. Do: Notify all those in the mandatory "reporting loop" of the allegation of patient abuse and neglect in a **timely manner** or as mandated by your respective state laws and regulations.

6. Do: Continue to provide In-Service Training to **all** staff relative to patient abuse and neglect and the responsibility of all staff to prohibit it, prevent it and report it in a timely manner. In my many years in this field it was more the norm for eye witness employees not to come forward in a timely manner and, at times, even mislead provider staff, the reluctance to report on a fellow caregiver or the infamous "code of silence."

7. Do: Always take photographs of the injuries/conditions subject to the investigation. It is well worth repeating here that I can't stress enough the importance and value of photographs taken of the victim's injuries and/or medical conditions that are the subject of the Internal Investigation. These photographs, especially if taken contemporaneously to the alleged incident, can be extremely valuable to any follow-up criminal investigator and to the prosecutor at trial. A nurse can take the stand and eloquently and professionally describe the patient's "black eye" and facial lacerations, or pressure sores, etc., but nothing has more profound impact on the jury than the photographs of an elderly and helpless vulnerable adult having sustained the photographed injuries or condition allegedly at the hands of a "caregiver." **Photographs should also be taken to record the phases of the injuries.**

8. Do: The photographs must be dated, timed, and signed by the staff person taking them.

9. Do: Conduct "private" interviews of witnesses and suspects. As we discussed previously, I don't have the skills of a nurse nor does the nurse have my skills as an investigator, but together we can make these procedures work after networking and cross-training.

10. Don't conduct the "interview" of a potential witness while standing at the Nursing Station or worse the "break room" for caregivers.

11. Don't conduct what I call "peanut gallery" interviews. These can be fatal to a criminal case. Over the years, I have seen good Internal Investigations explode into oblivion because during the investigations "management" saw fit for the interview of the suspect to be "attended" or "witnessed" by a number of, in my opinion, excess staff or, to be rather blunt, "deadwood" witnesses. The supervisor of the person conducting the interview "observes" and his/her supervisor "observes" and so on and so on up the ladder, thus the term "gallery." The prob-

lem with this is that they are not needed, they only complicate the documentation of the interview and finally, and most importantly, this situation is a potential windfall for the defense at trial. True case example of "real cases and real faces." We had a case in a rural western Maryland nursing home or Long Term Care Facility (LTCF) involving the alleged patient abuse (Assault & Battery) of a very elderly and incoherent (Alzheimer's) male patient.

During "AM Care" two female caregivers were in the room of the above-described vulnerable adult. A transfer from bed to wheelchair was to be conducted (Transfers are one of most frequent times incidents of patient abuse and neglect occur). One caregiver was much older and experienced than the much younger "new" CNA, who had only just been certified. The senior CNA was the suspect. The victim would not cooperate during the transfer, so the suspect employed, let us say, a form of motivation. The suspect took hold of the victim's nose and intentionally "twisted" it. The twisting was to encourage the victim's cooperation with the transfer. Of course, this technique will not be found in any CNA training manual. The young witness CNA had no advanced warning that the more experienced suspect caregiver was going to employ what amounted to an Assault & Battery upon the victim, and she was shocked and mortified. The twisting of the victim's nose would have been bad enough, but what the suspect did not count on was leaving very visible and bleeding injuries on and around the victim's nose. The suspect's finger nails came in direct contact with the victim's nose and surrounding soft facial tissue as she twisted. The results were devastating. The victim, as a direct result, sustained lacerations all around his nose following along the lines of the twisting motion. The suspect communicated very little with the young witness caregiver after the transfer was completed and as the victim was bleeding and weeping.

The two caregivers then proceeded to wheel the victim out of his room into the hallway past a Nursing Station on the way to breakfast. However, three Licensed Practical Nurses (LPNs), count them, three, were sitting at a Nursing Station and clearly saw the suspect with the young CNA as she wheeled the bleeding and weeping victim past them. As stated, all three LPNs saw the victim with the suspect and witness caregiver and, in unison, ordered the suspect to stop as they asked what had happened to cause the victim's injuries. The suspect then without hesitation uttered a very clear "admission of guilt" by telling the three LPN staff that it was okay, she only had to "pinch" the victim's nose in order to obtain his cooperation in the transfer. The three LPN staff then informed the suspect to leave the victim in their care, as they reported the incident to the supervisory RN on duty. This incident occurred very early during "AM Care" and most of the upper management level supervisors were yet to report to the LTCF. The three LPN staff members then did several very correct things. They assessed the victim's injuries and also photographed the injuries.

To all you professional law enforcement folks out there, you know this was looking really good so far in establishing "probable cause" to believe a crime had been committed. For you non-professional law enforcement folks out there, why? We had a witness to the alleged attack, we had visible and fresh injuries, and we had three professional supervisory staff witnesses to the visible injury and to the spontaneous admission of guilt by the suspect. We had photographs taken within moments of the victim sustaining the facial injuries. However, the case would begin a downward spiral from this point on. Why? Before for the morning was over and the suspect was finally ordered off the property pending the Internal Investigation and the notification of those agencies in the reporting "loop," the suspect, the eye witness, and the three LPN staff witnesses were interviewed multiple times by separate managers and each time with a growing and, as we have stated, unnecessary "peanut gallery" of other managers and supervisors in, shall we say, "attendance."

How could a case that started out so well "go south" so fast? It is clear to you. The multiple interviews of the eye witness, the suspect, and the three LPN staff witnesses totally confused the jury. Our office was notified in a timely manner, but not in time to prevent the fatal flaw errors. Regardless, we did proceed with a criminal case. Why? We proceeded because our legal staff thought it was the righteous thing to do, and the victim needed someone to stand up for his rights and in an open court of law. We knew the case had serious problems brought on by the aforementioned Internal Investigation, but our legal staff opted to proceed. I conducted several days of on-site work at the facility, meeting with management, reviewing and obtaining the appropriate medical records and Internal Investigation files, obtaining all photographs, meeting with the demented victim, more a courtesy than anything, and conducting our own formal interviews of the eye witness and the three LPN staff witnesses. I also conducted the interview of the suspect caregiver. Later, and prior to our placement of formal criminal charges against the suspect, two of our legal staff traveled back to the facility with me to meet briefly with the management, the DN, and our witnesses. This all demonstrated an extraordinary amount of commitment by our office.

We placed our formal charges against the suspect, who was later represented by the local Office of the Public Defender, who I must say did a fine job. You may recall earlier that I warned that the multiple interviews with multiple "peanut gallery" staff present could be a windfall for the defense and it was. In spite of our eye witness, in spite of the three LPN staff witnesses to the visible injuries and to the spontaneous admission of guilt by the suspect, and in spite of photographs of the injuries, and the other forms of evidence such as medical and administrative records, we did not prevail. This case was one of only three defeats our office suffered in over 11 years while I was the Patient Abuse Coordinator. Why did we not prevail? Many reasons really, all dealing with the fatal flaws of the Internal Investigation, but we really should have still prevailed. Unfortunately, the jury was totally confused over all the interviews and all the persons present each time. Our witnesses did not fare very well on the stand, in spite of all the attempts of our legal staff to rehabilitate their testimony. Now, I think you know why my stance against unnecessary multiple interviews with "peanut gallery" staff is so strong. The taste was indeed a bitter one. It was a very long ride back home to our Baltimore City office that day; my supervisory prosecutor and I were devastated. Suddenly, I uttered a spontaneous bit of humor, which fortunately for me was taken well, very well, by the prosecutor. I quoted a line from a country music song by Mary Chapin Carpenter. I said, "Look at it this way Tim, 'Sometimes you're the windshield, sometimes you're the bug.'" The prosecutor, who was not familiar with the great song, burst out laughing and it seemed to put things back into perspective. Our ride home went on a little better and we later continued working criminal cases as our office marched across the State of Maryland pursuing case after case with victory after victory in our quest to protect the vulnerable adults of our State.

12. Do: Have the witness submit a written statement and, if possible, in his/her own writing and words. If the witness asks the staff conducting the Internal Report to write the statement for him/her, this must be documented in a preamble to the statement and both persons must sign and date it with a third person also signing it. Before asking the suspect/witness to sign the statement, the interviewer should read the statement to the suspect/witness, word for word. There must be no misunderstandings.

13: Don't just merely hand the witness a blank sheet of paper and have the witness drop it by your office later. Wrong. I think we have discussed some of the real "jewels" I have encountered over the years such as "I don't know nothing." This was the entire written statement to an allegation of "witnessed" patient abuse, Assault & Battery.

14. Don't rule out the roommates of the victim as potential witnesses. Even if the roommates can not undergo the rigors of trial, that does not preclude them from providing helpful information during the Internal Investigation. Let the criminal investigator and prosecutor later decide the possible benefit or availability of the roommate to offer testimony at any legal proceeding. I can't tell you how many times during the interviews of suspects how referring to the victim's roommates paid off. I would simply say to the suspect in a very confident voice and demeanor that I had gathered records, taken photographs and also interviewed the victim's roommates! What I did not tell the suspect is that the roommates, because of mental and physical infirmities, could never testify against them in court. Yet, I had planted a seed in the mind of the suspect that I could use to my advantage. Another tactic I often used when interviewing suspects is to inform them that it would be much better for the truth to come out and to come out now. Of course, I didn't tell the suspect that while it "would be better," it would actually be much "better" for the later prosecution of the case.

15. Don't rule out other non-caregiver employees, such as housekeeping and maintenance staff, because they are all over the facility and, at times, can even seem "invisible." However, they see and hear much more than perhaps we will ever know.

16. Do: Notify the victim's family or responsible party in a timely manner and keep them informed as you progress through your Internal Investigation. Needless to say, follow any and all requirements set forth in your respective states.

17. Don't think that patient abuse and neglect can't happen in your facility, because, as we all know, it can happen and at any time day or night. Thus far in this book, we have discussed numerous "real cases and real faces" examples, such as defendants who have included an elderly visitor, a trained volunteer, an awarding winning and beloved LPN, sexual predators and just pure and simple thugs. Patient abuse and neglect will not stop. We can hope to diminish it, but beware it will always be just around the corner. I have seen it occur in inner city nursing homes and also the most expensive private-pay retirement centers.

18. Do: Follow the advice of your attorney, because that is why you have retained him.

THE BENEFITS OF A CORPORATE LEVEL INVESTIGATOR

Now that we have addressed "Internal" investigations of Incident or Accident Reports, I think one can see how complicated and time consuming such investigations can be to a nursing home or other caregivers such as those providing care for developmentally disabled adults. It has been my experience over these many years that even patient abuse and neglect involving a "simple" case of Assault & Battery upon the vulnerable victim can literally all but shut down the front office of the facility for days!

PROFILE OF THE CORPORATE LEVEL INVESTIGATOR

Who fits the "profile" for this position? Well let's see. The investigator must have extensive experience in law enforcement from the point of execution to supervisory and management levels. The position must have a person with extensive experience in the investigation and prosecution of allegations of patient abuse and neglect and other crimes. The person must have a proven "track record" that provides management and/or law enforcement with cases that can proceed to an administrative or criminal level adjudication. The person must also have the ability, and if I may say so, the "personality" to reach out and establish and then maintain professional rapport with others in the "loop." The person must be a team player. The person must never forget that he/she seeks the truth. The person should be able to stand and deliver interesting and informative training sessions to all levels of professionals in this field. He/she must have the ability also to stand and deliver while testifying before the Grand Jury and/or at criminal trials. I can't think of many other places on this earth where you are so totally on "your own" than sitting on stand at trial. I always found comfort in my prosecutor and the fact that I knew the "truth" was on the stand with me. Most importantly, the person must want the position and all the hard work, long hours and responsibilities that it requires for success. Why, in short, it would appear that this "profile" fits your writer! Perhaps after I come out of retirement, I will pursue such an opportunity.

The Federal and State governments have made it very clear that they both expect and even demand that more "corrective actions" be taken against facilities in which patient abuse and neglect allegedly occur. Having a "corporate level" Investigator under an operational wing, such as Risk Management, can address the general problem by conducting in-depth and professional Internal Investigations.

The position serves to protect the best interests of the respective facility and all the members it serves by establishing a structured, uniform, and professional system for conducting Internal Investigations of physical abuse, neglect, emotional and financial crimes committed against vulnerable adults. The position can also provide "corporate level" management with an Investigator free to conduct "internal corruption" investigations into allegations of wrong doing committed by managers and staff throughout the corporation.

The position provides a method of avoiding possible criminal and even civil litigations involving vicarious liability in hiring, retention, training and supervision, etc.

The position can be of significant advantage in providing assistance to the legal staff of the facility/corporation and to other management personnel. An issue such as patient abuse and neglect directly impacts the service of direct and professional medical care by the nursing and medical staff. If the allegations surround the alleged theft of facility property and/or any misuse or diversion of facility or corporate property, then the upper management of Facility Operations may be involved. This investigator position can also assist corporate level legal staff in looking out for the best interest of the corporation or the "Big Picture." However, I must say here very clearly that the position must not be compromised or influenced by upper management when it comes to any investigation but especially, investigations of allegations of patient abuse and neglect. Nor should the relationship the investigator must maintain with outside professionals, such as government regulatory and law enforcement agencies, be compromised.

The investigator position should establish a professional rapport with others in the "loop," the State Health Department, The Department of the Long Term Care Ombudsman, the police, and the respective State Medicaid Fraud Control Unit.

Some states, such as Maryland, have enacted laws that require care providers to conduct Criminal Background Checks on all direct care staff and others in the facility. In short, and thankfully, the days of "thugs" going from facility to facility with their "Certification" in hand and being "hired" literally on the spot, are numbered. While an outside contractor can provide assistance in obtaining the Criminal Background Checks, both locally and nationally, the corporate level investigator can conduct more in-depth investigations into individual Applications for Employment. You may recall this is one of the most profound negative effects a facility can experience. Hiring an employee, even after a successful Criminal Background Check, without checking out critical entries furnished on the Application for Employment can spell trouble later. Just because the person does not have a "criminal record" does not mean he/she has not been accused, investigated and terminated for suspected or alleged patient abuse and neglect. Look for entries relative to "blank" periods of employment. Why? The Applicant could have been fired for suspected patient abuse and neglect, but it never went forward to criminal prosecution or other forms of "formal" adjudication. Therefore, as I have stated earlier, it may be necessary for the investigator to "refresh" the applicant's memory. Finally, Human Resources professionals will tell you, that while significant progress has been made, at times the applicants are not fully investigated due to time and financial restraints. This issue could be one of responsibilities assigned to the corporate level investigator.

The investigator, who fits the above-described "profile," can and will after time also generate revenue for the corporation. Yes, I did say generate revenue. How? Training. The corporate level investigator can have standard and professional lesson plan formats for presentations not only for the respective corporation, but also outside agencies and other care provider staff. There are never-ending possibilities, such as the In-Service Training of Nursing Staff, training of other facility management staff, government agencies, such as the Long Term Care Ombudsman, and State Health Department, and even law enforcement agencies. As for training law enforcement professionals, I remain a Certified Instructor at the Federal Law Enforcement Training Center, and I can tell you the training cycle will never end either at the in-service level or the recruit academy level. The corporate level investigator can provide this training to other private sector facilities for a reasonable fee. It is a never-ending need. Also, please remember that if you retain an investigator fitting my suggested "Profile," he/she, because of his/her respective prior experience in the patient abuse and neglect world, will have a "rolodex" full of contacts in the professional regulatory and law enforcement fields.

This corporate level position can, in time, meet all the above-mentioned needs, plus the position can represent a positive image for the entire corporation. For instance, corporate level staff can consider a "Press Release" informing the public of their commitment to the investigation and, most of all, prevention of patient abuse and neglect. In short, be "proactive" and take a "positive" stance.

The position can take the heavy and, at times, unrealistic burden off the shoulders of the individual facility and release the management at both the administrative and nursing or care levels to go about the most important business of caring for their patients. For those of you out there who are administrators or managers of nursing homes, you fully know and have experienced how just one allegation of patient abuse and neglect occurring in your facility, sustained or not, can literally "close down" your front office management for days. You must first deal with the Incident Report or Internal Investigation, then the victim's family, the various local and state regulatory agencies, and finally law enforcement, not to mention the "press." All that, and you have still not completed the journey. Why? What if the case proceeds to formal criminal charges? You have the subpoenas to deal with, the cost and manpower to produce copies of all the records requested; most times opposing legal staff waives the "best evidence rule" and allow "copies" of medical records for trial. However, this is not always the case especially when key relevant medical records from the chart are presented at trial. Many manpower hours are lost as management and nursing staff are committed to testify at trial. The "corporate level" investigator takes much of the burden off the local facility while, as I have already stated, assisting the corporate legal staff representing the corporation.

Lastly, since this is a "corporate-wide" position, and the investigator does not answer to any one facility management, he/she can be the independent "eyes and ears" of the Corporate Officers.

9

Prevention

My constant refrain over these many years has been, and I respectfully hope you know by now, "Patient abuse and neglect can happen in any facility and at any time." That said, we can still "prevent" incidents of patient abuse and neglect. By "we" I refer to private citizens, law enforcement, and government regulatory agencies, such as the Department of Health, Long Term Care Ombudsman and even the nursing homes and other providers of care to our vulnerable adults. Perhaps, we may never be able to chart or calculate the actual incidents prevented because of the cold hard fact that these incidents often go unreported or late-reported. We also face difficulty in gathering accurate statistics since they are often calculated using various different "definitions" of patient abuse and neglect across our nation. However, once again, we can still prevent some incidents and we must be persistent and consistent in our efforts to do so. If we prevent "one" incident of patient abuse and neglect, it will be worth the effort. In short, prevention it is a never-ending cycle.

Prevention at the Nursing Home or other "Provider" levels

Providers can start "preventing" incidents of patient abuse and neglect at step one, during the hiring process. Yes, before the potential abuser is even hired. How? The provider must have high standards and then be consistent in meeting and maintaining those standards. The provider, if not already required by state law, must conduct criminal history checks on all caregiver staff and other staff as required. As stated, this must be done whether the respective state has a law or regulation requiring it or not. You may recall my previous example of "real cases and real faces" when we discussed a well-known and respected nursing home administrator, who kept a "tall stack" of returned positive criminal history checks on his desk. Why? He kept the criminal history checks, which, by the way, are expensive, especially when you run both local and national checks, on his desk and in plain view to remind him of how the money was well spent. The "tall stack" of direct caregiver applicants included individuals who were convicted felons and some even fit the definition of "career criminals." I can attest to this in more than one case, but I can tell you that one of my early suspects was an "18 time loser." Yes, indeed, I said an "18 time loser." For those of you non-law enforcement types out there, the suspect caregiver, who was accused, investigated and later successfully prosecuted by our office, physically attacked three vulnerable adults on just one 11:00 p.m. to 7:00 a.m. shift. Two of the vulnerable adult victims sustained visible injuries with one sustaining a broken finger. The caregiver was previously convicted on 18 different criminal charges. Needless to say, this case took place before the State of Maryland passed legislation requiring that nursing homes and other providers of care to vulnerable adults conduct criminal history checks on frontline caregivers and other specified staff.

The effort for the passage of the law was spearheaded by our then Attorney General J. Joseph Curran, Jr., members of his legal staff, and other respected leaders including at least one administrator of a nursing home. Yes, as you can guess, it was the administrator who conducted criminal history checks before our law requiring it was passed. I was also honored to testify in support of the Bill that was later passed. This was no easy task, because a significant number of facilities and provider organizations were against the Bill because of the costs of running the criminal history checks, especially the national checks. Our arguments were simple and direct. We live in a very mobile society with Americans moving and relocating not only locally but nationally. Of course, we, as do other states, have the simple fact of "geography" on our side. Take the State of Maryland for example. In the western part of our state one can nearly walk across the state lines of Maryland, West Virginia, Virginia and Pennsylvania. The eastern part of our State is bordered by the states of Delaware and, again, Pennsylvania and Virginia. We also have the fact that Washington, DC is surrounded by several State of Maryland counties. Just south of Washington, DC is again the State of Virginia. Applicants can literally walk across some streets and be in the State of Maryland. Thus, one can clearly see why national criminal history checks are an absolute must in the never-ending battle to prevent patient abuse and neglect.

Providers **must** consistently be diligent in the review and verification of all Applications for Employment and resumes. Why? We have previously addressed this, but applications contain a myriad of information. This information has a long established history of being embellished, exaggerated and outright falsified. Provider Human Resources professionals have even acknowledged the fact that applications are not investigated as thoroughly and consistently as they would like. **The point here is that if you don't hire a problem, you won't have a problem, pure and simple.**

Providers or other care facilities must have very clear Policies and Procedures prohibiting and mandating timely reporting of patient abuse and neglect. The facility must enforce them! All staff must also "sign off" on the respective Policies and Procedures.

Training, training and more training. The providers must have, as part of the never-ending cycle of "In-Service Training, a block on patient abuse and neglect. The providers must also conduct formal training for supervisory and management staff. Why? This staff is responsible for the facility in the end and also responsible for conducting internal investigations of these allegations. These internal investigations can, as we have stated, be solid building blocks for any follow-up investigation. Unfortunately, if poorly conducted, they can also be nearly useless to the criminal investigator.

Provider management and supervisory staff must reach out to law enforcement also including the Medicaid Fraud Control Unit-Patient Abuse Coordinator, the State Health Department, and Long Term Care Ombudsman and even the families of the patients under their care in order to seek assistance and input in recognizing and reporting allegations of patient abuse and neglect. In short, management must be proactive, not merely reactive, to prevent incidents of patient abuse and neglect. Once again, it comes down to establishing professional relationships, training and more training.

Providers must openly welcome suggestions by government regulatory agencies, such as the State Health Department Surveyor Units, the Long Term Care Ombudsman advocates, and law enforcement on how to better protect the vulnerable adults under their care. These protocols must remain consistent and continuous, not just following an incident of alleged patient abuse and neglect or a poor Survey.

Open your eyes and ears to the fact that patient abuse and neglect, in spite of all our positive efforts to curb or stop it, will continue to occur. We can all reduce it but, regrettably, never totally stop it. It is often very "spontaneous" and it is all too often unreported and/or under-reported in general. I have seen it and felt the negative effects of it numerous times over these many years. As I have stated, that is not to say that there are not many good and even loving caregivers out there at all levels, because there are. I have seen them and spoken with them often. There are good and loving frontline caregivers out there with, in some cases, 20 years or more of award-winning performance. However, this fact means nothing to the coherent victim of patient abuse and neglect or to his/her loved ones who must leave the patient there day after day and night after night under the constant threat of possible patient abuse and neglect. We also have the unfortunate fact, which we have addressed previously in this book, that acts of patient abuse and neglect are sometimes committed by highly regarded and honored caregivers and professional staff, such as RNs, LPNs and Medical Staff.

Prevention at the Law Enforcement level

Awareness and training: The police must understand that the patient abuse and neglect of vulnerable adults are indeed crimes. If you don't have a specific criminal cite you still have many other forms of criminal laws, such as Assault & Battery, and the various degrees of sexual assault, and reckless endangerment, to name just a few. These are crimes against those citizens the agency staff have been sworn to protect. Law enforcement staff must come to **consistently** realize that there is absolutely no difference between a crime occurring in an apartment complex involving an Assault & Battery and an allegation of patient abuse and neglect occurring within a nursing home or a provider of care such as those who care for our developmentally disabled adults. For you see, they have been sworn to **protect all citizens** within their respective jurisdictions. Please, I remind the reader that I'm a retired detective sergeant who also worked the "road" before my various promotions and, thus, know the pressure of going from "call to call" as your sergeant on the radio tells you to get it done and get "back on the road." At times, it seemed we were "professional report writers" and not professional criminal law enforcement officers. Training and lots of it is needed and it will be never-ending. The crimes of patient abuse and neglect are not going away and, in fact, will only increase. Why? As we stated earlier, two words, "Baby Boomers." The "Baby Boomer Generation," my generation, will flood the care provider world within the next two decades. Of course, this means more vulnerable adults and, thus, sadly, more potential victims. The training cycle for police must start in the Police Academy and continue throughout the police officers' careers in the form of "In-Service Training" and other specialized training, as appropriate.

Cross-training with other professionals responsible for the investigation of allegations of patient abuse and neglect: The police must establish a professional rapport with others responsible for protecting vulnerable adults. I speak specifically of the State Health Department, the Office of Long Term Care Ombudsman, and the Medicaid Fraud Control Unit of their respective states. Not every state has a Medicaid Fraud Control Unit or the same commitment. Specifically, 47 States and the District of Columbia have MFCUs. This cross-training will, I can assure you, benefit not only the police but all those in the professional "loop."

I have repeatedly referred to the absolute necessity for establishing and maintaining professional rapport for a reason, it works!

Law enforcement must, through continued cross-training and networking, become "more comfortable" operating within "nursing homes" or other care settings. Many police officers simply just don't like investigating crimes occurring inside these types of facilities. This has changed for the better over the years, but must continue to change. Once the police become more familiar with the nursing home or other care provider "worlds," the more comfortable and competent they will be investigating patient abuse and neglect allegations. We can go back to our "building blocks" analogy; a good basic and sound police report can build a solid foundation for follow-up investigators and for the prosecutor at trial.

Crimes occurring in nursing homes and any settings of care to vulnerable adults should be included within a specialized unit of the Police Department; I would suggest the Child Abuse Unit. Why? Look at the profile of the victims. They are both vulnerable, easily intimidated, often can not be reliable witnesses, and are also left right back in the environment in which the alleged abuse and neglect occurred as the investigation is being conducted. Also, the Crime Prevention or Police Community Relations Units should be more knowledgeable on the issues of patient abuse and neglect and, thus, be able to take part in presentations and awareness programs within the facilities. This knowledge is imperative when meeting with the citizens and loved ones of vulnerable adults. In short, have trained staff willing to educate citizens on how to have a positive impact on preventing these crimes, just like your agency does for Breaking & Entering, burglaries, robberies, etc. Go to senior citizen centers, go to seminars, and visit long term care facilities as part of the never-ending in-service training programs.

Prosecution of criminal cases of patient abuse and neglect: Sometimes it will all come down to this, the grand finale so to speak, or the ultimate "action taken." This is not just the suspension or termination of a suspected abuser, but the prosecution and, when appropriate, incarceration of the convicted abuser. Not all patient abuse and neglect cases are "opened," not all cases go beyond the preliminary investigative stage, not all cases reach the Grand Jury level, and finally, only a very few, about 10 %, ever end up on the criminal case docket in a court of law. I can tell you from speaking with the frontline caregivers, those most often charged in these cases, that the criminal prosecution of a fellow caregiver does have a profound effect. I also recall some administrators, who would cut out our press releases and the newspaper stories covering the trial and/or conviction of an accused patient abuse and neglect defendant, and then actually tape them over the "time clocks" so caregivers saw them day in and day out. Extreme?

Think about it. Is it more extreme than sexually abusing three coherent vulnerable ladies? Is it more extreme than cutting costs in a facility to the point that illnesses spread like an epidemic wild fire, and pressure sores rocket to Stage IV causing vulnerable adults to undergo amputations? Is it more extreme than a mentally and physically vulnerable adult female being victimized by being forced to perform a perverted sex act on a "visitor" to the nursing home? Is it more extreme than a caregiver intentionally leaving several blind, deaf and profoundly mentally retarded vulnerable adults completely alone and unsupervised while they all sat around a large bowl of food? How dehumanizing! And worse, the apartment, in which the caregiver completely abandoned the vulnerable adults, catching fire? Is it more extreme than another caregiver intentionally leaving five vulnerable adults alone and completely unsupervised as she went to pick up her boyfriend who was 45 minutes away, one way. And again, after she left the five vulnerable adults alone and completely unsupervised, the group home catching on fire because of her careless placement of scented candles used to cover up the smell of urine? When the Fire Department arrived, one of the vulnerable adult victims was still sitting on the commode because she needed assistance with personal care. I can go on and on, but the answer would still be the same, no. No, not at all. Prosecutions and the follow-up public information sources are the very least we can do to protect our vulnerable adults.

Prevention at the Regulatory Agency levels

First of all, I must say this, if it had not been for the sincere cooperation and efforts our State Health Department (Maryland Department of Health & Mental Hygiene), and the State Department of Aging-Long Term Care Ombudsman Program, then our efforts (Office of the Attorney General-Medicaid Fraud Control Unit) to establish a patient abuse and neglect unit would have seriously faltered, if not stumbled along the long and dusty road we started back in 1989. I sincerely personally thank them.

Both of these agencies are doing, in my opinion, an overall outstanding job in their respective efforts to protect vulnerable adults in the State of Maryland. However, that is not to say that we can not always seek to do better. Both agencies are understaffed and underpaid. Additionally, the Long Term Care Ombudsman Program can not perform its role without all their volunteer citizen staff. Both of these agencies must continue their never-ending work literally "within" the facilities. Simply put, their respective oversight and monitoring. State Health Department surveyors, who again while under staffed, must not fall into the all too human fault of following into a mundane "rut" of going from nursing home to nursing home merely going through the motions, so to speak. Facility management should not be at the door waiting for the surveyors and their "unannounced" inspections.

Surveyors have a difficult job interpreting and then enforcing the myriad of Federal and State regulatory cites. The Federal Government beats the drum to which the states must march. The regulations seem to change like the blowing of the wind from one year to another and one federal administration to another, thus, making the job of the nursing home surveyors, who are trained professionals, all the more difficult. However, the surveyors must, and I have personally experienced it first hand, continue their difficult missions without becoming discouraged. Nobody said it would be easy. Right?

Both of these agencies must continue their respective "outreach" and training efforts with law enforcement. As we have stated in this book, the outreach and training of law enforcement is a never-ending cycle and an absolute necessity. The effort should start at the Police Academy level and continue through the In-Service Training of law enforcement personnel. Please, I understand the overwhelming burden of staffing this commitment places on these truly overworked agencies. However, the positive benefits can be enormous.

Also, understand that I'm not suggesting that these regulatory and monitoring agencies have the necessary staffing to "personally" train every police officer in their respective state. However, these agencies can provide on-going training to key training personnel within each major agency. These agencies can meet with the police department management and arrange to formally train personnel of the police academy and in-service training units on the state agencies' respective roles and how law enforcement can contribute to the effort of protecting our vulnerable adults. In short, hand the ball off to another team player and let them run with it. Of course, this will mean, and it is a good thing, continuous and consistent networking with the training personnel to assure that they are provided the correct and up-to-date information. I would suggest the benefit of an occasional visit to a class by a representative of the respective state agencies. It will also provide the opportunity for the regulatory agency staff to actually speak "one on one" with police officers. Over these many years, police officers have come a long way, but still need to improve and be more familiar with the caregiving "world," so they can protect all those they are sworn to protect, even those in nursing homes and other caregiving facilities. They can accomplish this and then consistently maintain their familiarity of the caregiver world by being provided training by the professionals of the Long Term Care Ombudsman Program and respective Health Departments.

Prevention at the private citizen level

Yes, even private citizens can assist in the active and on-going prevention of patient abuse and neglect of our vulnerable adults. How? Awareness, education, volunteer work, and interaction with government regulatory agencies, such as the State Health Department and Long Term Care Ombudsman Programs and private advocacy entities, such as the local chapters of the Alzheimer's Association[1] and the National Citizen's Coalition for Nursing Home Reform (NCCNHR).[2]

As for the private entities, a word of explanation seems in order. The Alzheimer's Association provides continuous information and training on the signs and stages of Alzheimer's disease and publications in addition to their support group efforts. The Alzheimer's Association states their goals as "To eliminate Alzheimer's disease through the advancement of research; to provide and enhance care and support for all affected; and to reduce the risk of dementia through the promotion of brain health." I can speak personally regarding Maryland's Alzheimer's Association and their fine work as I have seen it over these many years. Also, in 1997 I was honored to have been the recipient of the "Glenn L. Kirkland Award" which is only presented to one person yearly by the Alzheimer's Association.

The NCCNHR brochure states, "We are consumers and advocates who define and achieve quality for people with long term care needs." NCCNHR's mission is to accomplish quality through informed, empowered consumers, effective citizens groups and ombudsman programs, best practices care delivery, public policy responsive to consumer needs, and enforcement of consumer-directed health and living standards."

The local office of the Long Term Care Ombudsman program also offers the opportunity to private citizens to take part in awareness and training seminars. This can be especially valuable to those with loved ones in the various settings of long term care. Various awareness associations, such as those we have mentioned, also offer suggestions and brochures on how to evaluate a particular facility setting or nursing home. My suggestions are simple and direct; if you must soon place a loved one in a facility, go there first! **Ask to review the latest results of the State Survey Report.** This is public information and the report should be easily available for the citizen's or loved one's review. The Survey Report, of course, does not list the actual names of patients nor should it ever have!

---

1. National Alzheimer's Disease and Related Disorders Association, Inc. Hotline # 1-800-272-3900, e-mail: info@alz.org

2. NCCNHR Phone # 202-332-2275, Address: 1424 16th Street, N.W., #202, Washington, DC, 20036-2211.

The survey report clearly lists the findings of the particular survey. It is an absolute must for loved ones to be aware of and review this survey prior to the admission of the patient into a Long Term Care Facility. For additional details I suggest you contact your respective State Health Department and/or local Long Term Care Ombudsman Program. I also suggest you ask the tough questions of facility management. Why should I place my loved one in your hands? What is your performance record? Do you have Policy and Procedures prohibiting abuse and neglect of your patients? Do you have investigative procedures? Have you had any incidents of alleged patient abuse and neglect? If so, what type and what was the end result? Do not only ask the tough questions but also look over the facility for yourself. Open your eyes and really "look." Frankly stated, **look, listen and even smell. Yes, I said smell.** There is no good reason why you should walk into the facility and be hit smack in the face by the overpowering smell of urine! At times dog kennels are less offense. This is especially clear when you go from one facility to another and get slapped in the face by the disturbing odor in one facility but not in another! Why? If the respective facilities both care for the same patient profile, such as a number of patients suffering from urinary incontinence, then why should one facility slap you in the face with odor and not the other? There are numerous reasons all dealing with care. Are the patients provided personal care in a timely manner? What happens to the discarded diapers and the soiled linens? In short, as we have addressed, I can think of no reason why this condition should occur.

Once your loved one is actually admitted, don't become a stranger to the facility! Even if your loved one suffers from some sort of mental disability, such as the many forms of dementia and Alzheimer's disease, still visit. I understand how painful and also how time-consuming this effort can be, but it is a "good thing" to do. I have even seen families accomplish this by having a visiting schedule within their family. Know the names of the caregivers assigned to care for your loved one. **Also, let them know you know their names.** Take part in activities in the facility and keep up with the survey performance of the facility. Take part in you loved one's "Care Plan" meetings periodically conducted by nursing staff. You must be proactive and not merely reactive. This is not meant to be all inclusive and I respectfully suggest you make contact with your local Long Term Care Ombudsman advocates and your other government regulatory agencies for additional information.

We have previously addressed, in my opinion, the often "forgotten" victims of patient abuse and neglect, the developmentally disabled vulnerable adults. I have provided numerous "real cases and real faces" examples of my criminal investigations and later criminal prosecutions by our Assistant Attorney Generals of defendants accused of abusing and/or neglecting these vulnerable adults. Victims suffering from the various forms of mental retardation and physical disabilities also have various monitoring, regulatory and advocacy agencies. I suggest you check with your State Health Department or Department of Social Services for additional information. There are others, such as the Association of Retarded Citizens (ARC), which is a national non-profit association. ARC provides care for developmentally disabled adults and has thousands of group homes and other forms of care centers over the United States. In the State of Maryland alone ARC has approximately 5,500 members. The listing of ARC in this book is in no way or manner intended as a personal endorsement for placement of your loved ones under ARC's care. I mention it only as a possible resource for the loved ones of developmentally disabled vulnerable adults. There are numerous advocacy groups throughout America. I suggest you check the internet for additional information.

Lastly, I recommend citizens, advocates and other government agencies take advantage of the opportunity of contacting their respective state Medicaid Fraud Control Units (SMFCUs). As stated, 47 States and the District of Columbia have MFCUs. We have already addressed the benefits of having a MFCU and the proud history SMFCUs have in the protection, investigation, prosecution, and prevention of patient abuse and neglect. I suggest you check out the U.S. Department of Health and Human Services web site for additional information on the SMFCUs.

In summary, as we have seen, the effort to prevent incidents of patient abuse and neglect of our vulnerable adults falls on many shoulders, the government, private sector and finally individual citizens. For in the end you see, we all must protect our vulnerable adults. Why? It is the very least we can do.

There are over 17,000 nursing homes caring for over 1.5 million of our loved ones in the United States. This does not include the many thousands of developmentally disabled adults out there in thousands of facilities, such as "group homes" and larger care settings. This number excludes the thousands of elderly vulnerable adults kept "upstairs" in the back bedroom." Sadly, these cases often don't come to the attention of the authorities until it is far, far too late. The ambulance medical professionals arrive to a call of an "unresponsive" elderly family member only to find that the victim suffers from severe malnutrition, dehydration, and has developed Stage IV pressure sores. It is the responsibility of all of us to protect our vulnerable adults.

10

Things to Remember on the Road to Success

In this chapter we will address general suggestions that will assist you in the never-ending efforts to combat the "beast" that is patient abuse and neglect of our vulnerable adults. I will provide you with some of the overall steps to success that have worked for me these many years. We will also briefly summarize by listing some of the most common threads of the fabric it will take to create and then carry the "banner" into battle. "Banner," a word I first used back in 1989 when I presented the legal staff of Maryland's Office of the Attorney General—Medicaid Fraud Control Unit with my written report, which was more a formal proposal. It was also revolutionary in a way since it proposed the absolute necessity that our office be prepared not only to investigate and, when appropriate, prosecute patient abuse and neglect cases now and again, but be proactive not reactive. We would have to seek out criminal cases and not be content just to merely receive a referral "now and again." It was a report that would lead to the creation of the permanent Patient Abuse Coordinator position and to the commitment to the mission of our office combating the patient abuse and neglect of our vulnerable adults statewide from the Eastern Shore and Ocean City to the ski slopes of the Western Maryland mountains and all in between. I can tell you that I will never forget the opportunity, the challenge and the reward this commitment has provided me.

"Banner," a word I said to any one who would listen. Yes, the Office of the Attorney General—Medicaid Fraud Control Unit would be the very "first" to create the colors of the banner, pick it up, and carry it into the battle. This investigative and prosecutorial "banner" is still held high and still in the hands of Maryland's Office of the Attorney General—Medicaid Fraud Control Unit. It is also time to pass out some additional "banners" to those who are willing to take on the challenge and come with us and others such as the Long Term Care

Ombudsman, State Department of Health & Mental Hygiene, law enforcement, and other prosecutorial government agencies across our wide and diverse country. Yes, we are a diverse and yet strong country. Again, while we are diverse and patient abuse and neglect are many things to many people, the "beast" is still there no matter what our respective state laws call it or label it. We are also a country noted for our overwhelming generosity to others in need. While this is certainly a good thing, it is also time we show true compassion to the needs of our vulnerable adults. Can there be a more noble cause?

We have previously addressed some of this material in earlier chapters; however, some topics are well worth a summary review. I have also provided some additional material. So let us proceed.

SOME SUGGESTIONS ABOUT INTERVIEWS AND CASE NOTES

We have previously addressed "Case Notes" and the importance of them, but here we will address some additional suggestions. Once again, I remind the reader I'm not an attorney and you must follow the advice of your respective legal staff. I can tell you that the information provided here is based on methods that have withstood the test of time and court challenges and simply put, they work for me. You must do what works for you. There are entire books out there addressing various investigative and interview techniques. Here we will simply "cut to the chase" and list suggestions and, at times, explain just why they work. Most of the suggestions apply to all those professionals responsible for the investigation of allegations of patient abuse and neglect. All of them pertain to criminal investigators as they deal with the ever-present "Miranda Warning."

The interview of a witness or suspect must remain under your control. Remember, you are in charge and not the other way around. You must have an agenda and, while the interviewee may attempt to impose his/her own agenda, it is you who must prevail. It does not matter your respective professional status, from administrator, to DN, to regulatory investigator, to an experienced criminal investigator. You beat the drum that sets the agenda and pace of the interview. This is not to say that there can't be informative exchanges during the interview. However, it still all goes back to the basics. **When all is said and done, you call the shots.**

The "Miranda Warning," we must address it yet again. Use it when you must, use it when instructed to do so by your legal staff, and finally don't use it when it is clearly not required. I can tell you that in all my years in law enforcement I was never challenged in open court regarding issues over the "Miranda Warning."

Paramount in discussions regarding your "case notes" is that they must reflect the truth. Should you like to pursue a career in crime fiction novels, fine, but no creative writing here!

Your notes must be in your "own hand." I remind you we are not addressing a case summary report or other memorandum, etc., that are routinely produced by a word processor. We are speaking about the notes you keep during an interview that can lead to the solid foundation analogy or the demise of your case.

The case notes must be dated, signed, record any and all breaks, record the beginning and ending times, record any and all other persons present during the interview and the length of time they were present. Most critical is the signature of the witness or suspect. Sounds extremely basic, right? I can tell you I have seen many documents lacking the signatures!

If you are a criminal investigator, your notes should be included in a section for "Case Notes." **Don't commingle your interview "case notes" with other case records because should the defense subpoena records they may be caught up in a wide net and released.**

Don't ever get caught in the line of fire between your prosecutor and the defense. They have more fire power than you.

Your "Case Notes" to file must be in the original form and in ink.

Accurate case notes are also critical for non-law enforcement professionals tasked with conducting Internal Investigations into allegations of patient abuse and neglect. Regulatory investigators must also learn to keep accurate case notes. These can not only be critical to any administrative actions taken against an individual caregiver suspect but also the facility, should systemic violations of patient abuse and neglect be detected. When the administrative action has been completed and a criminal investigation follows, the various regulatory investigative agencies should expect a call from the criminal investigator and/or the prosecutor. Why? Think of the potential evidence contained in the regulatory investigation files and records of adjudication. The possibilities are almost endless. One example is that the records may contain such evidence as written statements that, when compared with those gathered during the follow-up criminal investigation, are found to be conflicting. Other examples are any and all records of testimony provided during the Administrative Hearing. Once again, the records may contain conflicting statements that follow-up criminal investigators and prosecutors may find very informative.

Remember, your case notes can and most likely will end up in the hands of the defense! We have no fear when we seek the truth and do our very best "in good faith" to document the results in our case notes. If this not the case, be prepared for the defense to come down on you and to come down on you hard! This does not include residual consequences such as internal investigations and administrative actions that may follow against you.

When another party reads your case notes, they should follow much along the lines of the typed memorandum formally documenting your interview. Your case notes and the typed memorandum should run parallel to each other as to times and events recorded in the interview.

Since you are not a machine, your case notes will be in the form of short "bullet" phrases and perhaps some sentences here and there. **Keep it short, but also keep it accurate.** Remember, as you are writing your case notes you are also making eye contact with the interviewee and attempting to "read" responses. Ideally, you will have someone taking notes so you can devote your full attention to the subject of the interview. However, in the overwhelming number of my cases, I hunted alone.

Policies of tape recording interviews or interrogations vary from agency to agency. In the case of the Maryland Office of the Attorney General, it was our policy not to tape record these interviews. Again, this is a decision for the legal staff. I have seen it work, but I have also seen witnesses, during my career as a detective sergeant with an agency that had a policy permitting the employment of tape recording, "clam up" at the very sight of a tape recorder. That is not to say that it can't work, because, at times, it can.

Quotes! If the suspect makes a spontaneous admission of guilt then document the admission of guilt word for word. Why? Just picture yourself on the stand as the defense is verbally slapping you around as the attorney attacks your case notes and the veracity of your entire testimony. Of course, for those law enforcement professionals out there, we know that the interview and spontaneous admission of guilt are hopefully followed up by a complete and detailed written statement or confession.

You should have a prepared list of points to be covered during your interview and document at what point during the interview you actually addressed them. Don't have this prepared list as part of your actual case notes, but keep it as an aside to refer to at your leisure during the interview. As you proceed in your interview and cover the respective point, just "cross it off." This "aside" list of points should also be dated and signed by the note taker.

Document in your case notes the actual time during the interview that the suspect utters any spontaneous admissions of guilt. This is simply done by placing the time and date next to your notes documenting the admission of guilt. Why? Why not? This is just another method of the accurate documentation of your interview. You can also refer back to it during the interview to counter other statements especially any inconsistent statements the suspect may utter after the previously documented admission of guilt. It works.

When conducting interviews I don't like to hear too many of the below phrases:

"To tell you the truth …"
"To be honest with you …"
"I swear to God!"
"I really can't recall."
"I don't remember."
"I can't remember." (I often confront the suspect by saying, "Which is it? You "don't" remember or you "can't" remember?")

Of course, this list is not all inclusive and we all utilize these phrases and others similar to them. I'm not implying that these phrases can't be uttered under honorable circumstances. However, I can tell you that when you are conducting an interview and such responses repeatedly follow "key points" of your interview, then such repeated responses are often defensive maneuvering or posturing by the subject of the interview. I often keep a little log aside recording the phrase and when it was uttered by the subject of the interview. Later, I often confront the subject of the interview regarding the phrases he/she uttered and the amount of times the phrases were said. If the timing is right and the interview appears to be "going my way," I confront the subject by saying that it is my opinion, that every time he/she said to me, "To tell you the truth," it was followed by deception. Hey, if the timing is right take the shot. Is this an exact science? No, it is not, but I can tell you at times it can be an effective tool.

Do **not** willingly provide the subject of the interview with a copy of your interview case notes. This is clearly a matter for your legal staff to address with the defense. I might add, do **not** provide the subject of the interview with any documents or reports.

What do you do if the subject of the interview starts taking his/her own notes during the interview? Nothing, you do nothing. You can still control the agenda of the interview. As for the notes taken by the subject, they are merely the subject's notes, nothing more and nothing less. I do suggest that you record in your interview case notes that the subject told you that he/she was taking the notes. If the subject does not actually tell you he/she is taking notes then just make a record of the fact that during your interview of the subject it "appeared" he/she was taking notes. Of course, don't be surprised if the notes taken by the subject of your interview conflict with your notes!

What do you do if the subject of the interview breaks out his own tape recorder advising that he/she intends to record the interview? This is a tough one. Hopefully, you will already have a policy or directive from your legal staff on how to best address this matter. If not, it is your call. I never personally encountered this situation. Some factors to consider would be: Is it a witness or suspect interview? How difficult would it be to relocate and interview the subject of the interview? What phase of the investigation have you reached? What have you obtained from other witnesses? If you lack legal direction and have to make a decision "on the spot," I would utilize my interview finesse to attempt to persuade the subject of the interview that the use of the tape recorder would be counterproductive. If that failed, and I could not obtain advice from one of our prosecutors, I would consider the use of the tape recorder by the subject of the interview as a violation of the "rule" that I must control the interview and not the other way around. I would advise the subject of the interview that I would not conduct the interview under these circumstances and our office would be back in touch to reschedule and that the new interview date may not be exactly at the convenience of the subject of the interview. What is the bottom line in all this? Hopefully you will have a directive from you legal staff as this is clearly a matter for their attention. If not, make the decision and make the tough calls on your own.

Brief Summary—Interview Techniques and Case Notes

You must control the interview and not permit the interviewee to control it or impose his/her own agenda. Case Notes are the foundation upon which the formal documentation of the interview is built. Your case notes must be accurate and most importantly, they must be the truth and documented in good faith. Case Notes to file must be in your own hand and signed and dated by you. Don't provide the subject of the interview with a copy of your case notes. In fact, don't give the subject of the interview anything! A good rule to follow in your mission is to obtain information and not to provide information to those outside your office. **Don't commingle your case notes with other notes or documents in your case file as they may be caught in a wide net subpoena issued by the defense.**

Coordination of efforts to combat patient abuse and neglect

A repeated refrain throughout this book has been that all the parties in the "professional loop" for the care, protection and advocacy of vulnerable adults must establish and maintain a professional rapport with one another. It is well worth repeating here, because it works. I have been involved as a team player in establishing and then maintaining professional rapport and I have seen first hand the positive results that follow. Professional rapport is more than a friendly conversation during a seminar or convention or handing out business cards. To work it must be deep and sincere. I always have the direct lines of my fellow associates in the "professional loop," and they mine. I also have a consistent policy of returning phone calls! When I present training and advise those present to call and/or page me and I will get back with them, I do. This simple courtesy alone can have a profoundly positive effect. We should not have to jump through red tape and unnecessary protocols in order to contact each other during a crucial point in an investigation of patient abuse and neglect. The sooner the Department of Aging—Long Term Care Ombudsman, the Department of Health, and law enforcement, to include the 47 states and the District of Columbia, which have Medicaid Fraud Control Units, establish professional rapport, the sooner they can get down to the business of protecting our vulnerable adults. This "coordination" plays an enormous role in the efforts to combat the patient abuse and neglect of our vulnerable adult citizens.

When does patient abuse and neglect happen? As we have stated, it happens in any facility and at any time. While there are countless examples of this fact and we have addressed many of them in this book via the "real cases and real faces" examples, here we will discuss yet another. Along with our legal staff, I took part in a Friday afternoon training session we conducted in a Washington, DC nursing home. Just to illustrate, as I stated to the attendees my signature phrase that "Patient abuse and neglect can happen in any facility and at any time," I looked down at my watch and stated it was occurring in some facility at that very moment. The next day, a Saturday, I was called on my cell phone by the administrator of the nursing home that hosted the training session the day before. The administrator advised me that her facility had patient abuse occur on the very afternoon we presented our training to staff. This case was successfully prosecuted by former Special Assistant U.S. Attorney Alexis Taylor. Yes, patient abuse and neglect can happen in any facility and at any time.

Pressure sores can and must be avoided. Pressure sores can result from lack of proper hygiene, hydration and positioning and turning. They can also result from contributing secondary medical conditions and end-of-life medical conditions. Pressure sores can be a direct result of the long standing and systemic patient neglect of vulnerable adults. Another factor that can "trigger" the development of pressure sores is the lack of proper staffing. The lack of proper staffing directly contributes to the "triggers" leading to the development of pressure sores.

What are some of the "triggers" contributing to incidents of patient abuse and neglect? One of the "triggers" is also, as above, the lack of proper staffing to adequately provide care to the patients. The lack of frontline caregivers such as Certified Nursing Assistants (CNAs) directly impacts the incidents of patient abuse and neglect. If the CNA has too many patients and not enough time, this equals patient abuse and neglect. Please notice I did not say possibly, I said "equals." When staff feel the pressure of too many patients and not enough time to provide care, then watch and see how the injuries of unknown origin and the rate of pressure sores increase. Patients are not provided personal care such as assistance in toileting and diaper changes in a timely manner, patient hydration and hygiene care drops, and witnessed incidents of patient abuse and neglect occur, and go unreported or under-reported. Low self-esteem can also contribute. If a CNA goes from day to day, week to week, month to month and year to year with no significant additional training and no hope for upward mobility, he/she fits the profile of a potential abuser. Of course, none of these factors excuse any criminal acts.

We all know that patient abuse and neglect can happen in any facility and at any time, but we also know that it often occurs during normal activities of care. Incidents or "triggers" leading to possible patient abuse and neglect occur during personal care, such as assistance in toileting and diaper changes. It occurs during "positioning and turning." It occurs during assistance while eating. It occurs during transfers. It occurs when a caregiver intentionally ignores the call for assistance from a patient as the patient sits in his/her own urine. It occurs when caregivers intentionally deny the patient access to his/her call button by throwing the call button on the floor. It happens when developmentally disabled vulnerable adults are routinely left unsupervised and, thus, placed in danger. It occurs when the facility management intentionally cuts back on the "tools" for care, such as proper staffing and durable medical equipment (DME). It occurs after the facility management inadvertently hires "thugs" after failing to conduct in-depth inquiries into Applications for Employment. It occurs when sexual predators in the form of "visitors" and "volunteers" roam the hallways looking for and finding victims. It is occurring as I write this book and it will be occurring as you read this book!

Summary and other things to remember

1.   The Patient Abuse Coordinator **must want** to be assigned these cases.

2. The prosecutor should also **want** to prosecute these cases.

3. Develop "forms," such as the "Suggested Checklist," that will assist you and others in "the loop."

4. Train and take part in cross-training.

5. You must control interviews!

6. Take accurate "Case Notes."

7. Written Statements must be signed by the interviewee.

8. Do not conduct "peanut gallery" interviews (mere observers).

9. Limit the amount of interviews conducted.

10. Conduct your interviews in private; don't conduct them at the Nursing Station!

11. Law enforcement officers, use "Miranda Warning" when you must.

12. Ideally, a registered nurse should be a member of any Patient Abuse Unit.

13. **Always take photographs** of injuries or conditions, such as pressure sores!

14. Always meet with the victim. At least provide them with that courtesy.

15. Don't forget about roommates as possible witnesses!

16. When interviewing elderly witnesses be sincere, be patient, don't fire off rapid questions and show true compassion (It won't hurt you, I promise.).

17. Nurse Managers, beware of a pattern or increase in "injuries of unknown origin."

18. Providers of care for our developmentally disabled vulnerable adults, be vigilant in your supervision and monitoring of "group homes." Make frequent and **unannounced** visits to your facilities. I guarantee this will have a positive effect on your efforts in the detection and prevention of patient abuse and neglect.

19. The unannounced visits to group homes for our developmentally disabled vulnerable adults should often occur during late evening hours and on all holidays.

20. Managers of all care facilities must be aware and **proactive**, not reactive, to all forms of patient abuse and neglect.

21. Administrators must have clear and concise Policies and Procedures addressing the issues of patient abuse and neglect and mandate that employees sign off on them.

22. For those of us with loved ones in the various types of care facilities, visit often, know the names of the caregivers of your loved ones and let them "know you know them." Ask management the tough questions. Open your eyes, ears and noses and be observant.

23. Make contact with and maintain a rapport with your local Long Term Care Ombudsman Office. These people, who are most often volunteers, are very well versed on all matters relating to the myriad of State and Federal regulations that care facilities must follow. They are true advocates for the patients.

24. While we all must be diligent in the protection of our vulnerable adult loved ones, there are over 17,000 nursing homes alone out there. Although my career has been spent investigating and hunting down criminal abusers, I must tell you that the vast number of caregivers out there are doing a fine job. Also, administrators and nurse managers are well educated professionals, who, at most times, are very helpful to me and others in my profession during investigations.

25. However, and as I have repeatedly warned in this book, because I **must**, even the very best and well-trained administrator or nurse manager, can not and will not prevent all incidents of patient abuse and neglect. It is the "nature of the beast," if you will.

26. Proper number of staffing is basic; the lack of adequate staffing equals patient abuse and neglect. Pure and simple.

27. Stop patient abuse and neglect incidents before "they" enter your care facility. Human Resources (HR) staff must consistently and thoroughly investi-

gate all Applications for Employment in order to avoid hiring "abusers." In short, prevention starts at the HR door.

28. Conduct Criminal History Checks on all your direct caregiver staff and others as deemed appropriate. Conduct these Criminal History Checks at both the State and National levels. We are a very mobile society, not to mention geographical proximity considerations. Conduct these checks whether you have a state law mandating it or not. In the long run it will be well worth the costs.

29. Loved ones and responsible parties for patients in nursing homes must be familiar with the Survey Process and the Survey Reports.

30. Nursing home management and/or corporate level management should assign specially trained staff to conduct Internal Investigations of patient abuse and neglect. This specially trained staff can also act as the liaison between the facility and the various outside regulatory and criminal investigatory agencies.

Suggestions for witnesses taking the stand

You may recall earlier in this book when we discussed how very lonely one can feel while on the stand in an open court of law. It can be a very lonely place indeed. You must know that you are not really "alone," if you have "truth" on the stand with you. You can also look into the eyes of your prosecutor for additional strength or guidance. However, in the end you must "stand and deliver," so to speak. Some suggestions I can offer are the following:

1. Listen carefully to each and every question.

2. If you don't hear or understand the question, ask the questioner to repeat it. If you are hearing impaired then inform the court.

3. Don't anticipate what will be asked or try to figure out where the questioning is going. Stayed focused.

4. Answer only the question asked. Don't "volunteer" information, especially on cross-examination.

5. Be truthful!

6. Be courteous and respectful!

7. Don't argue with the lawyer questioning you. You will not win that battle; the attorneys have bigger guns than you.

8. Don't get angry. Some examples: The questioner can and will be sarcastic at times as a simple tactic. The questioner will also intentionally mispronounce your name. The questioner will repeatedly, as another tactic, address you by an incorrect title or rank. For example, you worked very hard over the years to obtain a supervisory position as the Director of Nursing and the questioner refuses to acknowledge your position. Again, nothing personal, it is just a tactic. The questioner may not want to "elevate" you or your testimony via correctly addressing you by your official and hard earned management title. This tactic can be applied to any title or position including law enforcement titles or ranks. We all know that there is a significant difference between a young just-sworn police officer and a seasoned Detective Sergeant. Once again the questioner often avoids addressing your official rank or position. The questioner can be a master at stopping just at the point of displaying open disrespect, but again, don't expect any compliments! If so, watch out for the very next sentence the questioner utters, since it will be an attempt to discredit you and any testimony you offer to the court. Again, this is not personal, nor should it be, so just deal with it.

9. Don't carry anything with you on the stand unless your prosecutor or the court authorizes it.

10. If shown a document, look at it very carefully and read as much of it as you need to before answering any questions regarding it. Take your time!

11. Never ever guess while on the stand. If you honestly don't know, then you honestly don't know.

12. If the question requires a yes or no response, then answer yes or no. However, this is not to say that you can't attempt to explain the question beyond a yes or no response. Look to your prosecutor for guidance. However, don't appear to be evasive. Not good at all.

13. If possible, avoid such phrases as "In my opinion," "I think," or "I believe." However, if the court has recognized and determined your "expert witness" status, then "in my opinion" would be appropriate.

14. In most cases, look directly at the questioning attorney. However, there will be opportunities when, while answering a question, you should look at the judge and/or the jury. After a while you will even be able to comfortably scan the jury making eye contact. In time, you will find one or two jurors who seem receptive to your occasional eye contact. All this is not an exact science, but with experience it can work.

15. Don't become overly concerned in or attempt to interpret exchanges between the attorneys and the judge. Just concentrate on your testimony.

16. This is so very basic, but you must dress appropriately.

This book acts as an outline on how to detect, how to investigate both at the criminal and regulatory levels, how to present evidence to prosecutors and even how to prevent patient abuse and neglect. But it also provided me a venue to share with you some of my memoirs. Memoirs of the long, and, at times, lonely and dusty road of my law enforcement career. However, I must also tell you that I would not change a thing. The challenge and rewards of the roads I took are beyond the words of this writer. You may recall earlier in this book when I called for others to come join us and pick up additional "banners" in the never-ending battle against patient abuse and neglect. For you see, there can never be enough "banner holders" in this battle. The battle has been tough enough already, but beware the "Baby Boomers" are just around the corner from flooding the nursing home—Long Term Care Facility (LTCF) "world." Today, we care for our vulnerable adults who served our country during World War II, the generation that literally saved the world. Tomorrow, another wave of vulnerable adults awaits our professional care and diligent protection. So, come, pick up one of the "banners" and join us! It will bring you rewards and joy beyond words.

Joseph S. Bostwick
Summer 2007

The Patient Abuse and Neglect of Vulnerable Adults
Sources and Credits

1. The case notes of Joseph S. Bostwick, Patient Abuse Coordinator (Ret.), Medicaid Fraud Control Unit—Maryland Office of the Attorney General.

2. The Federal Law Enforcement Training Center Lesson Plans of Joseph S. Bostwick, Certified Instructor (National Association of Medicaid Fraud Control Units)

3. The Federal Law Enforcement Training Center Lesson Plans of Certified Instructors Joseph S. Bostwick and David L. Carman (Ret.), formerly of the Delaware Medicaid Fraud Control Unit.

4. Informative websites as appropriate

5. "Consumer Reports," September 2006

6. U.S. Government Accountability Office Report (GAO-07-241) March 2007

7. "Provider" (American Health Care Association), May 2007

8. "National Pressure Ulcer Advisory Panel" (NPUAP) Spring 2007 Newsletter.

9. "NPUAP Updates Stages of Pressure Ulcers." (Vol.21) Joyce Black, President.

10. Edition 20 of the Taber's Cyclopedic Medical Dictionary (Decubitus/Pressure Ulcers).

Disclaimer

The depictions and opinions described in my book are presented in good faith and to the best of my memory and ability. They are based on my own long law enforcement career, training, experiences, notes, lessons plans and, as stated, to the best of my memory. Although I proudly reference both the Maryland Office of the Attorney General and the Washington, DC Office of the Inspector General, in no way does this book represent any views or opinions of those respective government agencies.

Joseph S. Bostwick
Summer 2007

APPENDIX A

SUGGESTED PATIENT ABUSE/NEGLECT INVESTIGATION CHECK-LIST

Date of incident: _____

Time of incident: _____

Time first reported: _____

Person first reporting/discovering injury or condition:_____
_____

Floor/Wing Room Number:_____

Name, age, DOB, of the VICTIM:_____
_____

VICTIM: (Primary Diagnosis) MDS:_____
_____
_____
_____

Injury sustained to the victim: Yes:_____   No:_____

Injuries of unknown origin: Yes:_____   No:_____

Photographs taken: Yes:_____   No:_____
Note: Always take photographs!

If yes, by whom: _____

Attending physician and phone number: _____

Roommates of victim? If so name them and primary diagnosis:_____
_____
_____

Responsible Party/Family (Phone numbers) (Admission Sheet):_____
_____

List of staff working at the time of incident: (Assignment Sheets of Wing/ Floor, etc.) PLEASE INCLUDE TITLE: CNA, NA, LPN, RN, ETC.
_____
_____
_____
_____
_____
_____
_____

SUSPECT: Full name, title, DOB, SS#, address and phone #:_____
_____
_____

If SUSPECT is an "agency" or "temp" employee, please provide name of agency and phone #:_____
_____

List date/time agency notified and name of person notified:_____
_____

WITNESSES: Full name, title, SS#, DOB: address and phone numbers:____
_____
_____
_____
_____

WHAT OUTSIDE AGENCIES HAVE BEEN NOTIFIED AND WHEN?
Police notified: Date:_____ **Time:** _____
Report#:_____

D.H.M.H.—O.H.C.Q.: Date:_____ Time: _____
Name:_____

LTCO: Date: _____ Time: _____
Name:_____

OFFICE OF THE ATTORNEY GENERAL
MEDICAID FRAUD CONTROL UNIT
PATIENT ABUSE UNIT: Date:_____ Time:_____
Name:_____

Name/Title of the person completing this Checklist: Please print and pro-
vide phone number: _____

Date Checklist was completed: _____

Joseph S. Bostwick 2006 (rev.)

APPENDIX B

FACILITY RECORDS
PATIENT ABUSE/NEGLECT INVESTIGATIONS
(Some facility records of use to criminal investigative agencies)

(List is not meant to be all inclusive)

The Internal/Incident Report

The "Suggested Checklist"

The MDS of the victim

The Admission Sheet of the victim

Progress Notes (both nurses & physicians)

Skin Charts (pressure sores)

Bruising/Injuries of Unknown Origin Reports/Charting

Dietary Records

Meds Sheets

Social Worker's Notes (often very well written and also informative)

Assignment Sheets (Staff assigned to and around the reported/alleged victim)

Application for Employment for the suspect (helps you locate suspect, etc.)

Training Records of suspect (Did suspect sign off on specific training/care plan, etc.)

Performance Records of suspect—both positive and negative

ANY AND ALL WRITTEN STATEMENTS FROM STAFF (Originals best)

ANY AND ALL WRITTEN STATEMENTS FROM SUSPECT (Originals best)

A copy of the facility "Policy/Protocols relative to Patient Abuse & Neglect"

MRDDA Victims/Cases: Psychological Evaluation of the victim (level of MR, etc.)

Letters and other communications to the suspect relative to alleged incident

Joseph S. Bostwick 2005 (rev.)

Appendix C

Obtain a copy of the Internal/Incident Report

Obtain any and all written statements submitted by the suspect(s) and witnesses

Obtain a listing of employees and correct titles

The DN—Director of Nursing should be able to assist you in your investigation and furnish most of the information from the medical chart/record of the victim (MDS, family information, etc.). The Director of Nursing is often the ultimate supervisor of medical staff who may be suspects and, thus, able to provide information regarding the suspect's performance, etc. In short, the DN is you key point of contact.

Some staff employees or witnesses may be "agency" or "temps," who are not actually employed by the facility. If so, make sure you obtain the name and number of the agency and the correct job title of the suspect.

If possible, review and ask for copies of the nurses/physician's Progress Notes

Always meet with your victim, unless a doctor or other authority orders otherwise. Give the victim the courtesy. It will also provide you with the opportunity of documenting the appearance/condition of the victim at that time and for the record.

Know as much about the victim as possible before you attempt an interview (Is the victim demented, deaf or blind, etc.?).

Always … Always … take photographs of the victim's injury/condition and also describe them in your written report

Don't forget or rule out roommates as possible witnesses (Obtain MDS, etc.).

Attempt to conduct an interview of the suspect (Once they leave the facility you must locate them out in the community.).

OUTSIDE AGENCIES

Office of Health Care Quality—(State Health Department—DHMH)—This unit monitors and inspects nursing homes and other facilities. It also has a unit that investigates allegations of abuse or neglect and other forms of poor care for possible administrative adjudication.

Long Term Care Ombudsman (LTCO)—Every county has offices of LTCO. Ombudsman advocate for nursing home residents and their families. By law they also respond to allegations of patient abuse and neglect.

Office of the Attorney General—Medicaid Fraud Control Unit: Since 1989 the MFCU of the OAG has had a dedicated statewide effort to investigate and prosecute allegations of criminal patient abuse and neglect and has successfully prosecuted numerous cases.

Joseph S. Bostwick 2005 (rev)

Acronyms

ADL-Activities of daily living
ALF-Assisted Living Facility
AG-Attorney General
AAG-Assistant Attorney General
ARC-Association for Retarded Citizens
ASA-Assistant States Attorney
BM-Bowel Movement
CMS-Centers for Medicare and Medicaid (U.S. Government)
CNA-Certified Nursing Assistant
DA-District Attorney
DDA-Developmentally Disabled Adults
DDA-Developmental Disabilities Administration (Maryland—DHMH)
DN-Director of Nursing
DHMH-Department of Health & Mental Hygiene (Maryland)
DME-Durable medical equipment (wheel chairs, crutches, etc.)
FLETC-Federal Law Enforcement Training Center
GAO-Government Accounting Office (U.S. Government)
HIPPA-Health Insurance Portability and Accountability Act
LPN-Licensed Practical Nurse
LTCO-Long Term Care Ombudsman
LTCF-Long Term Care Facility (Nursing Home)
MFCU-Medicaid Fraud Control Unit
MDS-Minimum Data Sheet
NCCNHR-National Citizens' Coalition for Nursing Home Reform
NPUAP-National Pressure Ulcer Advisory Panel
OBT-Over the bed table
OHCQ-Office of heath Care Quality (Maryland-DHMH)
PAC-Patient Abuse Coordinator
RN-Registered Nurse
ROM-Range of motion
SNF-Skilled Nursing Facility
SMFCU-State Medicaid Fraud Control Units

Glossary

Administrator—This person has the overall supervision and management of the facility.

Admission Sheet—This is the official medical record documenting the physical admission of a patient into a facility. It involves various medical documentations, such as, has the patient been admitted with pressure sores and at what stage? Has the patient been admitted having sustained injuries of unknown origin? The document also records information as to insurance issues and responsible party and family.

Alzheimer's Disease (AD)
* Ten Warning Signs of Alzheimer's Disease:

1. Memory loss

2. Trouble getting things done

3. Problems speaking

4. Getting lost

5. Poor decision making

6. Problems thinking

7. Putting things in the wrong place

8. Changes in mood or behavior

9. Changes in personality

10. Loss of energy

* Alzheimer's Association (www.alz.org)

Application for employment—These forms must be thoroughly investigated and entries confirmed by HR, since applicants often "forget" certain incidents and "embellish" others. These forms are another example of records that can be critical to criminal prosecution since, if the accused failed to properly complete all entries in detail or even truthfully, the prosecutor can introduce inconsistencies found in the application as evidence attacking the veracity of the testimony of the defendant.

Assignment/Staffing Sheets—These records document the assignments of staff to particular patients and/or to general duties and tasks. Some examples would be staff assigned to care for a number of patients, staff assigned as supervisors, and staff assigned to provide medications.

Care Plan—The plan of care for an individual vulnerable adult located in the official records of the facility. Nursing managers and staff must follow the "Care Plan" during the course of everyday care.

Checklist—Refers to the "Suggested Patient Abuse/Neglect Investigation Checklist"

Decubitus Ulcers—Pressure sores/bedsores—This form of skin breakdown develops due to lack of proper hygiene, hydration, lack of mobility, significant secondary medical conditions, and end-of-life conditions, but also systemic intentional neglect. Pressure sores/bedsores develop into four stages ranging from minor to life threatening in nature.

Dementia—This is a medical condition that causes patients to become confused and disoriented. There are many forms and stages of dementia, but generally it is an impairment of intellectual function that is usually progressive and results in interference with normal social and occupational activities. Thus, dementia results in serious malfunctions in activities of daily living (ADL). Patients with dementia are often susceptible to the various types of physical abuse and neglect.

Eschar-As stated in Taber's Cyclopedic Medical Dictionary, 20th Edition, "dead matter that is cast off from the surface of the skin, esp. after a burn."

Geri-chair—This is one of the most utilized DMEs in the various level care facilities. Basically, it is a "recliner" on wheels. This enables nursing staff to take patients with lack of mobility to other areas of the facility for care and/or social interaction with other patients. They can also be used improperly as a form of physical restraint.

HR—Human Resources

Incident Report/Accident Report—A form used by care facilities, such as nursing homes to report incidents such as accidents, injuries sustained to a vulnerable adult by another vulnerable adult, incidents occurring between caregivers and vulnerable adults both of an administrative/regulatory and criminal nature, incidents occurring between family members and visitors to vulnerable adults and injuries of unknown origin. Of course, clear criminal acts of any type committed against a vulnerable adult must always be documented in these reports.

Incontinence—This is the inability to control bladder or bowel movements (BM). These patients are at the apex of risk for the development of the various "stages" of pressures sores/bedsores. Why? These patients often lack mobility and thus develop all the "triggers" that can, without proper nursing intervention, lead to catastrophic levels of pressure sores/bedsores. The higher stages of pressure sores/bedsores can result in amputations and/or even death.

Internal Report/Investigation—These reports vary in format but normally contain the same information gathered by facility management following the "internal" investigation into allegations of patient abuse or neglect by staff. These reports are sent as mere notification or to follow up investigations by government agencies, such as the State Department of Health, the Long Term Care Ombudsman, law enforcement, and the respective Medicaid Fraud Control Units. If conducted and documented properly, these reports, along with police reports, can be the building blocks that lead to criminal charges, if appropriate, or be disastrous and useless due to fatal flaws.

In-service training—Mandated "in-house" training provided to all levels of nursing staff working in the various levels of nursing homes. Records kept by the facility on trainers, attendees, and curricula can become crucial evidence should an allegation of patient abuse and neglect rise to the level of administrative actions and criminal prosecution in a court of law. Example: Records that show that an accused caregiver signed off on a presentation relating to the identification, prohibition, and reporting of allegations of patient abuse and neglect.

Immobility—This is the inability to move around or ambulate without assistance. These patients are at the high risk level for patient neglect most often in the form of pressure sores since they often can't change positions in bed or even geri-chairs.

Injuries of Unknown Origin—These injuries are most often "found" to have been sustained to a vulnerable adult rather than reported when they actually occurred. They are most often the result of an intentional or unintentional act committed by a caregiver upon the vulnerable adult and not reported due to fear of disciplinary action and/or the placing of criminal charges. An example of unintentional injuries would be when a caregiver has an accident, such as dropping the patient to the floor. The caregiver then places the vulnerable adult back into bed or a geri-chair and intentionally fails to report the incident to nursing management. This can be medically catastrophic to the patient. The patient has been denied proper medical treatment and the caregiver has now committed a criminal act. However, a significant number of injuries of unknown origin can result from other incidents such as self-inflicted or "patient to patient" incidents of physical attack.

Minimum Data Sheet (MDS): This medical report is one of the most important records kept by the facility. It provides all the medical information and conditions of the patient. Some examples would be: Does the patient have mobility? Does the patient have limited range of motion (ROM)? Does the patient have Alzheimer's decease? Does the patient have pressure sores/bedsores and at what stage? These are just a few examples. The Minimum Data Sheet must be updated periodically or when there is a major change in the medical condition of the patient.

Miranda Warning—This must be provided to suspects by law enforcement personnel under the circumstances required by Federal law. The Miranda Warning is:

1. You have the right to remain silent.

2. Anything you say can and will be used against you in a court of law.

3. You have the right to talk to a lawyer and have him with you while you are being questioned.

4. If you cannot afford to hire an attorney, one will be appointed to represent you before any questioning, if you wish one.

5. You can stop answering questions at any time.

Miranda Waiver-

1. Do you understand each of these rights I have explained to you?

2. Having these rights in mind, do you wish to talk to us now?

Patient Abuse (per Maryland Annotated Code)—The sustaining of physical pain or injury by a vulnerable adult as a result of cruel or inhumane treatment or as a result of a malicious act under circumstances that indicate that the vulnerable adult's health or welfare is harmed or threatened. Patient abuse also includes the sexual abuse of a vulnerable adult. An example of patient abuse is the assault and battery upon a vulnerable adult. Some States, like Maryland, have legislation designating Patient Abuse and Neglect as both a misdemeanor (lower crime—lower penalties) and felony (higher crime—higher penalties).

Patient Neglect—(per Maryland Annotated Code)—Means the intentional failure to provide the necessary assistance and resources for the physical needs of a vulnerable adult including food, clothing, toileting, essential medical treatment, shelter or supervision. Some examples are intentionally failing to properly position and turn a patient under care, intentionally not providing the vulnerable adult with proper hygiene, nutrition or hydration. Another example is intentionally leaving developmentally disabled vulnerable adults unsupervised.

Progress Notes (of doctors and nurses)—These are the official day-to-day medical observations of care and conditions of the patient. They are for the record and must not be altered. Under certain special conditions "late entries" can be entered, but only after approval by nursing management.

Resident Rights—This term is often related to the 1987 Federal law, referred to as the "Nursing Home Reform Law." The law mandates "Resident Rights" for such actions as being informed, filing complaints, and participating in their own care. These rights also include privacy and confidentiality, dignity, respect and freedom, as well as the right to make independent choices and rights pertaining to transfers and/or discharges. For more detailed information I suggest you contact the National Citizen's Coalition for Nursing Home Reform at their website, www.nursinghomeaction.org. You can also call your local Long Term Care Ombudsman, who acts as an advocate for patients.

Restraints—Patients also have the right under law to be free from "physical" and "chemical restraints."

1. Physical Restraints: These restraints include anything that is attached to or placed next to the body of the patient that limits movement or access to other parts of the patient's body. Some examples of restraints are cloth ties (I have seen bed sheets used) placed on the legs and/or arms of the patient, wheelchair bars, or any other item that prevents mobility of the patient. (In some cases, nursing staff implemented these "restraints" as a form of supervision or monitoring of the patients to prevent them from leaving their physical location or sight.) Under certain medical conditions and after other methods have failed, physical restraints may be implemented, but only after a doctor writes an order.

2. Chemical Restraints: A chemical restraint is any drug or medication used for discipline or convenience of the caregiver, but not to treat a medical condition. A chemical restraint can only be employed after other care methods have failed and a doctor writes an order. For more detailed information I suggest you contact a Long Term Care Ombudsman.

Slough—As defined by Taber's Cyclopedic Medical Dictionary, 20th Edition, "dead matter or necrosed tissue separated from living tissue or an ulceration," "to separate in the form of dead or necrosed parts from living tissues," or "to cast off, as dead tissue."

Survey Report: This is the official record of the survey/inspection of a facility by Department of Health personnel. Most of the "surveyors" are nurses. The report documents many issues and/or conditions occurring in the facility. The report must be available for review by the families of the patients and kept in a location accessible to those wishing to review it. Of course, no actual names are used to identify the patients in the report available to the public. The patients noted in the report are identified only as Patient # 1, Patient # 2, etc.

Transfers (during normal care)—This is the movement by care staff of a patient to or from his/her bed or geri-chair. Transfers are risky to say the least. If not conducted properly, the patient can become seriously injured. Accidents occurring during transfers can often go "unreported" by caregivers, thus placing the patient at medical risk, which can lead to charges for "criminal neglect." As I have stated, and will always remind caregivers, don't become criminals just because you have an accident with the patient. It is better to face the nurse manager than a judge in open court of law as you hear the words "the State of so and so against you!"

Triggers-Term often used to describe the conditions or acts that lead to specific incidents of patient abuse and neglect. Example: Some "triggers" that contribute to the development of pressure sores/bedsores are the lack of proper hygiene, proper hydration, proper position and turning, secondary medical conditions and end-of-life medical complications.

Vulnerable Adult—(per Maryland Annotated Code) Means an adult who lacks the physical or mental capacity to provide for the adult's daily needs.

978-0-595-47187-4
0-595-47187-0

www.ingramcontent.com/pod-product-compliance
Lightning Source LLC
Chambersburg PA
CBHW020436290526
45785CB00002B/880